DARTMOOR TIN MINING

HISTORY & HERITAGE

Bruce Boulton

based on an original text by Mary and Jessica Walmseley

First published in Great Britain in 2021
in association with the Dartmoor Trust.
Original text © Mary Walmesley and Bruce Boulton 1982 and 2021
Historic photos © The Dartmoor Trust unless otherwise stated.
Additional text and design © Simon Butler and Freeland Media 2021

All rights reserved. No part of this publication may be reproduced, stored in a retrieval system, or transmitted in any form or by any means without the prior permission of the copyright holder.

British Library Cataloguing-in-Publication Data.
A CIP record for this title is available from the British Library.

ISBN 978 0 85710 132 7

DEDICATION
To the memory of Paul Oliver
generous benefactor to the Dartmoor Trust

PiXZ Books
Halsgrove House, Ryelands Business Park, Bagley Road, Wellington,
Somerset TA21 9PZ Tel: 01823 653777
Fax: 01823 216796
email: sales@halsgrove.com

An imprint of Halstar Ltd, part of the Halsgrove group of companies.
Information on all Halsgrove titles is available at: www.halsgrove.com.

Printed and bound in India by Parksons Graphics.

Foreword

This is the third book* in a planned series to promote the Dartmoor Trust by taking particular themes in which to showcase just some of the 30 000 photographs now held in its Archive and which are available to the public through its website at https://dartmoortrust.org.

Along with the work of the National Park Authority there are many smaller organisations and groups that dedicate their time to ensuring that Dartmoor remains a place in which the natural landscape, the lives of those who live here and those who visit, achieve a harmony in which the essential nature of the environment is conserved. The Dartmoor Trust is one such body, a charity that provides support for local projects and whose members and Trustees appreciate and care about Dartmoor. But in order to best care for the future we must also look to the past, and the Dartmoor Trust's Archive, from which many of the photographs in this book are drawn, provides this vital link to our history.

Tin mining on Dartmoor has left an indelible mark on the landscape, from the early tin streaming activity through to the later industrial workings. Remains of blowing houses, wheel pits and tinners' burrows are there in abundance, although those walking on the moor may not recognise them for what they are. This book will enhance the reader's enjoyment of the moor by bringing the early history of mining to life through the stories told and the many photographs included, from those taken by the earliest pioneers of photography to images captured within the last few years. These together exemplify the importance of our Archive in being able to compare the changes that have taken place on the moor in the past 150 years or so, and in recording mining artefacts that have long since disappeared.

The Dartmoor Trust's Archive is open to all. I encourage you to explore the Archive online, to add further information to existing images, or to provide photographs of your own. Should you wish to be involved I invite you to contact us at secretary@dartmoortrust.org. Dartmoor's future is in all our hands.

Lt Col. (Retired) Tony Clark OBE
Chairman. The Dartmoor Trust

*See also *Legendary Dartmoor Pubs and Inns* and *Railways Round Dartmoor* in this series.

Acknowledgements

First my thanks are due to Mary Walmesley for her permission to include and adapt the text from the original book *The Old Men of the Moor*, written and published by Mary and her mother Jessica in 1982.

Grateful thanks also to Ashley Hobbs for transcribing and providing a digital version of the original text for this new edition; to Neil Mercer for his early encouragement; Steve Holly for his observations and updates on the original text; Vernon Morgan for his help and advice; Lee Bray of the Dartmoor National Park Authority; and Tim Powell who provided access to Teignhead Farm. Phil Newman gave his consent to use material based on his book *The Dartmoor Tin Industry: A Field Guide*, for which many thanks.

My son, John, deserves special mention here as do all my friends and colleagues in the Kelly Mine Preservation Society, particularly David Allen for his important contribution, also Anne Payne of Manaton who pointed me in the right direction regarding publication of the new edition, and to Simon Butler for his professional skill in putting the photographs, drawings and text together.

Finally thanks to the Dartmoor Trust for their support in ensuring that this new and revised edition saw the light of day.

Bruce Boulton
Chudleigh 2021

Contents

Foreword	3
Acknowledgements	4
The Dartmoor Trust Archive	6
Preface to the New Edition	9
Introduction to the Original Book	11
Chapter 1:	
Part 1: History & Laws of the Devon Stannary	17
Part 2: Trade & Trade Routes	25
Part 3: Communications	28
Chapter 2: Crockern Tor: The Stannary Parliament	29
Chapter 3: Lydford: The Stannary Prison	41
Chapter 4: Ashburton: The Royal Manor	49
Chapter 5: Ashburton Tin	62
Chapter 6: Chagford: The Market of the Moor	75
Chapter 7: Tavistock and its Great Abbey	91
Chapter 8: Tin in the Tavistock Area	97
Chapter 9: Plympton: Birth of a Great Port	101
Chapter 10: The Photographic Heritage	118
Appendices	140-41
Bibliography	142

Opposite: The author's dog, 'Bramble', at Gobbett Mine, Hexworthy.

The Dartmoor Trust Archive

The Dartmoor Trust itself came about through the foresight of the Dartmoor National Park Authority which, in 1996, saw the advantages of an independent charitable body that, whilst championing the overall aims of the Authority, could undertake projects that were outside the statutory body's remit. Since that time the Dartmoor Trust, under the guidance of its Trustees, has provided financial support to a wide range of organisations and individuals, from restoration of ancient artefacts to major educational exhibitions. From the outset the Trustees were determined to look for a keystone project that would underpin the overall objectives of the Trust, establishing a permanent profile alongside its continuing support for local initiatives. And so the Dartmoor Trust Archive came about – today a sophisticated data platform providing easy public access to over 30 000 images.

Such successes are not achieved without dedication and effort behind the scenes, and alongside their work on other projects the Trustees found themselves engaged in promoting the archive to encourage wider public interest. To this end, in 2000, a book *Dartmoor Century I* was published based on the late Victorian photographs of Robert Burnard. The book was launched accompanied by a major exhibition of photographs, and a year later *Dartmoor Century II* was published to celebrate the addition to the archive of 2300 photographs from the Sydney Taylor Collection. This was followed by the digitisation of the Chapman Collection of 4000 photographs, dating from the Victorian period to the 1960s and, more recently, over 6000 photographs from the Worth Collection held in the Torquay Natural History Museum. The fact that the majority of these thousands of images previously existed in negative form only, many as fragile glass plates, made it almost impossible for the public to have access to them. At last, through carefully digitising each photograph, it was possible to reveal – often for the first time for many years – thousands of unique images of Dartmoor.

Robert Burnard's photograph of the Hartor valley looking north-east, taken on 27 December 1887. The photo shows the remarkable extent to which the river valleys of Dartmoor were transformed into industrial landscapes by the work of tin streamers.

Ruined engine house and mine machinery at Lydford from a watercolour painted in the 1880s by Louisa Honey.

Such work is not without cost, and while the Trust has been assiduous in working within constrained budgets, it has been fortunate in seeking and receiving various generous grants and donations in order to maintain and develop the archive, constantly adding new photographs and upgrading the site and data storage, as the technology develops.

Most recently a bequest of £40 000 was received from the estate of Paul Oliver (1927–2017) to whom this book is dedicated. As a professor of vernacular architecture, working through Oxford Brookes, he led parties of students on Dartmoor well into the last years of his life and published extracts on many aspects of the moor and its built environment. His generosity has enabled the Trust to digitise the recently donated Francis Lee Collection, comprising over 8000 photographs covering the major river valleys of Dartmoor, taken between the 1960s to the 1990s. A number of these photographs are included in the present work.

Remains of a tinners building above Fishlake, from the Francis Lee Collection.

Preface to the New Edition

I bear responsibility for the reappearance of Mary and Jessica Walmesley's *The Old Men of the Moor* which was privately published by them in 1982. Their edited text in this new and revised edition is complemented with the introduction of many photographs, mainly from the Dartmoor Trust Archive, with others from my own resources and from private individuals. But, other than for some updating and contemporary observations, I cannot in any way take credit for the original authors' informative history of the early miners and mining on Dartmoor's wild wastes, and of the Stannary towns which supported them in their industry. Their intention was to provide a background to the laws governing the work of the early tinners and to paint a picture of those 'Old Men' and their relationship to Dartmoor.

Additional information and the many illustrations included in this new edition are intended to give some further colour to the story. A great deal of detailed research has taken place since the original text was written and the readers are pointed in the direction of works by Sandy Gerrard, Tom Greeves, Tony Brooks, Phil Newman and the Dartmoor Tinworking Research Group, in particular. The bibliography included here contains details of their works and other relevant books.

As interest in our industrial heritage has become more to the fore, a final chapter has been included containing photographs from the Archive identifying more of the remaining evidence to be found on and around the moor itself, including photos of Kelly Mine, Lustleigh, where work is continuing to restore this former mine site to full working order.

Without the help and guidance of many friends and colleagues, and with the support and backing of The Dartmoor Trust's Archive, whose co operation rescued me from insurmountable difficulties, this revealing, most worthy and informative of books may sadly never have reached a new and wider audience.

Bruce Boulton
Chudleigh
2021

Opposite: A detail from Christopher Saxton's Map of Devonshire first published in 1575. It originally formed part of an Atlas commissioned by Lord Burghley, the first national atlas ever produced. Despite the detail elsewhere, Dartmoor itself is depicted as largely devoid of habitation, although the Stannary towns, Ashburton, Chagford, Plympton and Tavistock are clearly marked.

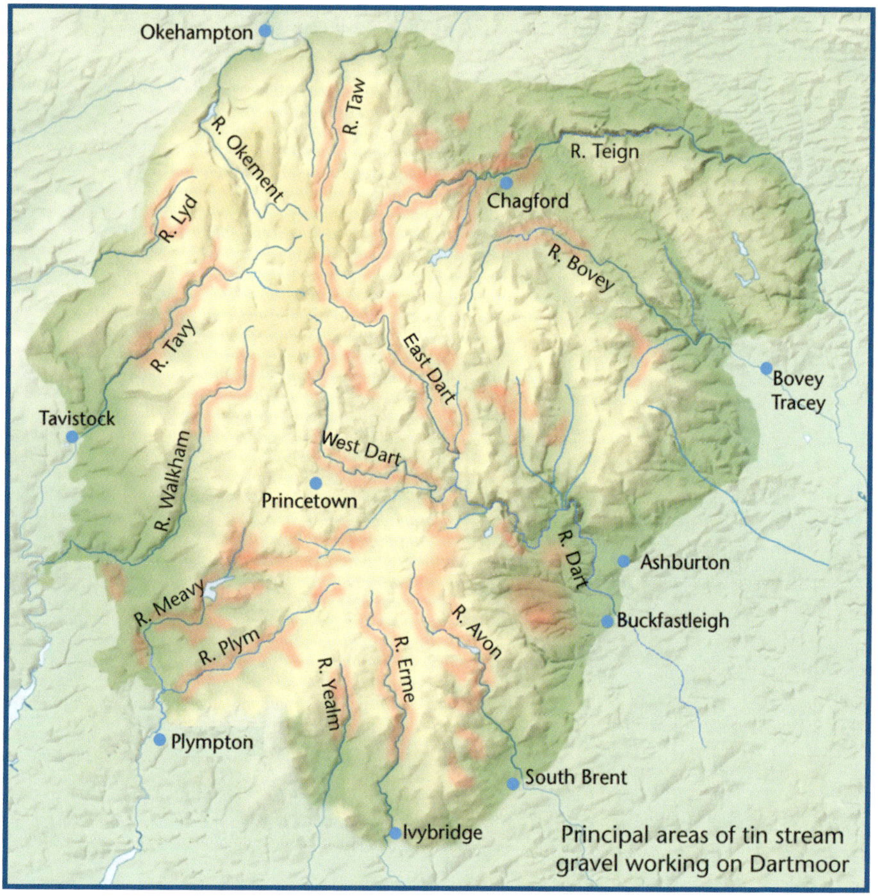

Principal areas of tin stream gravel working on Dartmoor

As the map above shows, there are few Dartmoor rivers and their tributaries that show no of sign tin streaming and much evidence is still to be seen today. The present day photo shows tinners' burrows (the mounds left as they worked over the stream beds) along the River Erme.

Introduction to the Original Book

Out of the window and across the valley, scattered farmsteads, a huddle of roofs round a church tower, woodlands, green fields cultivation; and beyond, on and up in the distance, hills, piling one above the other, veiled in mist when it is going to rain, hazy and shimmering in summer's heat; the last great wild region of the south-west – Dartmoor.

To the tourist it is Widecombe Fair, Haytor Rocks, the Prison or Dartmeet; a holiday destination visited by car or coach, or increasingly these days by bike. Many visitors don't leave the beaten track or stray far from the car park. For the more adventurous there are miles of open moor to explore.

From the first, my moor was different, for it was a frightening place. I had heard tell of quivering, treacherous bogs, of phantoms, and will-o'-the-wisps, of Dewer and his hounds, of fog that comes down like a blanket, of cromlechs and stone rings out of a secret past. I was fascinated and intrigued, and so also were the Victorians, who endowed the moor with a romantic image, peopling it with Druids and ancient deities who writhed and beckoned from every tor. But to the native moor dweller it is none of these things. They have lived and worked there all their days, and so have their forebears. To them, Dartmoor is a way of life.

In the eighteenth and nineteenth centuries writers and travellers such as Samuel Rowe, the Rev. J.P. James and Rachel Evans left us pictures of poverty and desolation, as depicted below in Samuel Prout's 1812 engraving of a dilapidated cottage near Chagford. Many of the families who built their houses on the moor, or established squatter's rights in the early Middle Ages, remained there for hundreds of years as smallholders and tinners, their way of life unchanged until the close of the last century. The moor men of those ancient days adapted themselves to their environment following a tough, crude

existence utilising the materials they found near their dwelling-places, becoming, at length, as hard and long lasting as the granite rocks upon which they lived. For though few of them inhabited the centre of the moor, this was not from a sense of fear; few of their legends tell of evil forces or malignant influences. Wrestling their way through life, ploughing and tilling the scanty soil, they became a part of the moor itself, and this identification is important when considering the attitude of the tinners to outside exploitation and interference.

This is not to say that Dartmoor was entirely a barren wilderness. As you will learn later in this story, it became in the Middle Ages a veritable hive of industrial activity. Beneath the heath and peat bogs lies the source of this former prosperity formed millions of years ago when that part of the earth's crust we know as Dartmoor was alive with volcanic activity. The tors we see today are the weathered remains of a great upthrust of molten igneous rock (a pluton) crystallized from magma slowly cooling below the surface of the Earth. The heat and pressure generated resulted in the numerous minerals, including tin, found both in the granite and surrounding geology. Over millennia, peat was formed on the high moor, springs gushed from the turf tumbling over the hills to the deep combes below, and forests of oak sprang up in scattered places. It was all there, tin ore, wood and peat for smelting and water to provide power. All that was needed was the ingenuity and knowledge to release the precious ore from the rock. The Old Men of the Moor provided that.

It is believed that in prehistoric times, stream tinning, the easiest and most primitive method of extracting ore, was first employed on Dartmoor. Stream tin is the metal ore washed down from the parent lode, and deposited in stream and river valleys. The quality of this ore is far superior to any found in a mine and appears to have been the only ore extracted in medieval times when, for a short period, Dartmoor was the principal producer in Europe.

The ancient rights confirmed in the Charters of King John, Henry III, and the first two Edwards all refer to customs relating to stream tinning; medieval documents always refer to tin workings as stream or moor works but never as 'mine

Wistmans Wood is one of three remaining ancient oak woods on the high moor. Timber, both for fuel and for construction was a vital commodity for early tinners and one they were free to exploit.

works', and when complaints of damage to crops or property were made against the tinners they invariably appear to have been caused by trenching and excavation of alluvial deposits and not by tunneling, adits or shafts.

Most of the prospectors seem to have lived on the edge of the moor, and the earliest workings would, of course, have been near their dwellings. But as the demand for tin rose, they extended their excavations up the valleys and into the more remote areas, occasionally building a rough stone shelter, or occupying the remains of prehistoric settlements. It is these distant tin workings that have survived, thus adding to the romantic image of the tinner, for the streams on the lower moor have been disrupted by cultivation. For many of these early miners, tin streaming was but one of their daily occupations.

William Pryce's *Mineralogia Cornubiensis*, published in 1778, provides a detailed account of streaming with many of the methods described being employed in earlier times. There remained a belief that deposits of ore had been left following Noah's flood, and after heavy rainstorms, when swollen rivers and water courses cut deep gullies in the valleys, so exposing these layers in pebbles and gravel, prospectors would search for signs of tin. Elsewhere tinners cut gullies along the hillsides thus allowing rainwater to wash down to the streams, exposing any ore beneath.

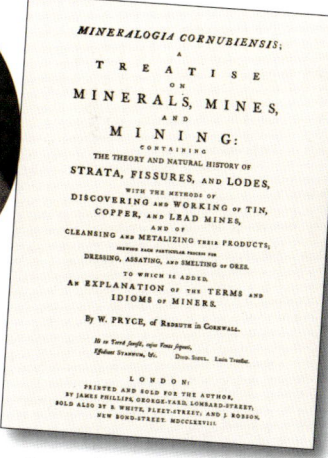

William Pryce's book is among the first major works on mining tin, lead and copper.

Besides these conventional methods of discovering tin, Pryce describes some of the more unusual methods, from dowsing with a metal rod to 'searching with uncommon eagerness the ground where Jack o' Lanterns have appeared', as it was believed that certain volatile compounds associated with tin gave off a flame seen as evidence of a mineral vein.

Identifying the tin ore was a skilled craft, heaviness, colour and a tinner's eye all being employed to work out how the ore had travelled and how rich it was in tin. When the tinner had decided that the ground was worth working he set up his bounds, this being the most ancient and important of his privileges. The following description of the procedure was written in the sixteenth century:

> *The manner of bounding is most commonly to make four corner bounds, two at the head of the work, and two at the tail, by cutting up three turfs in every corner, and then their head bounds and side bounds with three turfs in every place and laid directly against each other.*

Once he had 'pitched' a pair of bounds, the tinner was his own master.

The whole operation of stream tinning continued over a long period in a systematic and precise manner. During the winter months of greatest rainfall, the tinner dug the ore. With summer, came the washing and smelting process, great ingenuity being used to bring water to the tin-washing sites. Smelting in very early times was completed in two operations, first a rough drawing of the metal in a peat fire near the source of the ore, the tin being retrieved from the ashes in harsh, gritty lumps; later, a more careful refining at a recognised smelting centre. Dartmoor's Industrial Revolution can be said to have taken place in the thirteenth century, and tradition has it, that Jews were responsible for introducing mining innovations to the south-west peninsula.

Tales of spirits and wandering Jews* on Dartmoor are but folk memories of these enterprising merchants and businessmen who introduced new ways of using water power to work a bigger and more advanced type of furnace, thus giving sufficient heat to melt tin ore, and produce a pure metal in a single process. Pryce describes this in a vivid detail, calling the furnace 'the castle'. Probably similar furnaces, though on a smaller scale, were in use during the Middle Ages.

> *Tin and charcoal were laid in the castle, bellows throw in a steady stream of powerful air into the castle, which at the same time as it smelts the tin, forces it out through the hole at the bottom into a moor stone trough called a float, whence it is ladled into lesser troughs or moulds.*

For a furnace such as the castle it was necessary to employ a skilled warden who could be sure that it would remain stoked and burning by day and night, and who would also keep the bellows etc. in good working order.

The introduction of blowing houses meant important changes on the moor, and within the industry, for it is quite likely that whoever set up these blowing houses and financed the projects also paid the skilled men who maintained them, thus introducing a 'middleman' element, i.e. a person who was possibly getting more reward than the tinners themselves. Vast amounts of charcoal were needed to meet the demands of this type of furnace, and thus the peat charcoal industry began to expand rapidly over the northern part of the moor.

The way was now open for capitalists and profiteers, ready to invest in the opening of new tin streams, and this brought the Jews once again to the fore. With their expulsion in 1299, production fell, but in their place came Italian merchants, spelling loss to the small-time moorland tinner, for with them arrived an era of capitalism and foreign enterprise previously unknown.

The 'whole tin' that flowed from the blowing houses was as pure as any produced today, and it was destined to travel far. Most of the blowing house sites were near major pack-horse routes and, in those days, most of the manor houses

---

*Jews have a long and intriguing association with mining in Devon and Cornwall dating back to earliest times. This applied both to their expertise in mining and processing ore (in 1602, Cornish historian Richard Carew described tools being found in ancient workings including deer antlers, indicating a prehistoric origin from which all later mining developed), and to their vital role as money lenders supporting mining operations during the periods when usury was forbidden to Christians.

and many of the smaller farmers had, at least, one pack-horse of their own. Wheeled vehicles were not commonly used for transport on the moor. Everything was carried in panniers or on crooks (two pairs of willow poles bound and standing out from the sides of the horse). These carried the light loads; the heavy goods were pulled on 'truckamucks' (thick poles attached like shafts to the horses, and dragged along the ground), or on sledges.

The principal destinations to which the tin travelled, following its sale at the Stannary towns are listed in the Close Rolls of 1347 as 'Exeter, Topsham, Kenton, Teignmouth, Seaton, Sidmouth, Dartmouth, Brixham, Paignton, Kingsweare, Totnes, Portsmouth, Kingsbridge, Yelee(ne), Plymouth, Barnstaple and Bideford.' Tin was shipped and traded over long distances to Germany in the twelfth and thirteenth centuries. In the fourteenth century Bruges was the European centre for tin, though, together with wool, it sometimes went direct to Italy where merchants from Genoa, Florence and Venice were trading it from the thirteen hundreds onwards.

The Middle Ages proved to be a period of change, both social and economic. New ways of life emerged along with new means of utilising the soil and those who lived by it. With the Norman Conquest came a feudal society of lay and monastic landlords, manors and estates. Domesday Book provides evidence for thirty-seven manors with lands on Dartmoor. Also 195 'holdings' are known to have been on the moor at this date. There were many others outside the area, as well as the small settlements and villages such as that at Houndtor, which formed part of the manor of Tavistock.

Dartmoor now 'belonged to one man, the King of England who claimed to be free to do with it what he willed', for as a royal manor, Lydford included within that definition most of the moor itself. For two hundred years it became a royal hunting ground, a 'Forest', and families who had lived within its boundaries for generations were granted the 'privilege' of taking free fuel and pasture for a small fee. They were, however, subject to Forest Law which meant death for poaching offences.

As the twelfth and thirteenth centuries progressed, other foreigners began to arrive. These were the prospectors and adventurers who, searching for fresh pasture and for tin, settled in the 'Ancient Tenements', and the 'squatters' who, if

Between the rugged slopes of Greator and Houndtor lies a medieval village the remains of which are evidence of the layout of similar settlements once scattered across the moor.

they could build a house in a night, won freedom from their overlord. By the thirteenth century, many of the old commons, plains and wider river valleys had been enclosed, and crops were being grown at exceptionally high altitudes. Suddenly upon a wilderness, often shunned in turn by Iron Age people, Romans and Saxons, new horizons were opening for the people of the Middle Ages.

The Norman and Angevin kings skilfully exploited this encroachment upon the independence of the original moormen. Dartmoor belonged to the Crown, tin was a royal metal and the king upheld by charter the tinners' ancient rights, and backed them up in their fights against the landlords. Yet, when all was said and done, the tinners were also the king's subjects.

Little of the wealth that spread from the tin industry returned to the moor. Though Parish Guilds such as Widecombe, Holne, Chagford and Buckland invested funds in tin, and received gifts of the metal, this was but a pittance compared with the fortunes made by the king and those of his favoured servants who were granted permission 'to take all the tin of Devonshire and Cornwall for their own use'. Thus, the small-time tinner fell prey to the capitalist and the middleman, especially where, with the introduction of coinage in the thirteenth century, he received only one payment for his tin, at Michaelmas, and often found that he was pledging this in advance to tin merchants and adventurers. Ambitious entrepreneurs began to operate on a large scale, employing considerable numbers of men. So it came about that Richard Tregays who worked in tin near Plymouth was, in 1485, sued in chancery: 'Touching the ownership of 39 pieces of tin, he bought some, and dug and worked others by his workmen and servants.'

The tinners fiercely resisted accusations of trespass and damage to property, sometimes resorting to violence, and they made full use of the rights and privileges that the Crown had given them. Yet they were pawns in the game of king versus landlord, and in the long run, the old time tinner was bound to be the loser. At the close of the Middle Ages the moor and its people appeared much the same as in previous centuries. But gradually the tin stream industry was dying, and with its demise, there was nothing but the short-lived mining boom of the nineteenth century to take its place.

Lydford Castle is closely linked to the story of tin mining on Dartmoor. Edward I (r.1272–1307) appointed the castle as a Stannary prison. It held a fearsome reputation: 'A place of repute before the Norman Conquest and for centuries afterwards, it was the terror of the West'.

Chapter 1
History & Laws of the Devon Stannary

We do not know when they started tinning on Dartmoor, although as we have seen, there were streamworks near the Bronze Age settlements, and the recent excavation of the cist on Whitehorse Hill contained at least one tin bead among the grave goods which, though its origin is unknown, points to a long-standing local connection with the metal.

The discovery of a probable Bronze Age shipwreck off Salcombe on the Devon coast in the 1990s and its subsequent exploration revealed tin ingots among its cargo. This, and isotope data and trace element analysis of ingots recently recovered from a 3000 year old vessel wrecked off Israel's coast, appears to confirm Bronze Age trading links with Devon and Cornwall. These results, specifically identifying the origin of tin metal provide a major step forward in our understanding of early mining on Dartmoor and elsewhere in the South West.

With such evidence, conjecture that tinners have been exploiting parts of the moor well into antiquity now seems most likely and adds interesting possibilities to our interpretation of past events. For instance in the ninth century, Burghal Hidage records Lydford as being one of the burghs which defended tenth century Wessex from the Danes and, despite its isolated position, it was one of three Devon towns that boasted a pre-Conquest mint, in use from the reign of Æthelred II to that of his son Edward the Confessor.

The Kingsbridge estuary looking towards Salcombe and the sea, site of the Bronze Age shipwreck from which tin ingots were recovered. Inset: The 3000 year old tin ingots recovered from a wreck off the coast of Israel and identified as being from Devon or Cornwall. (© Ehud Galili).

Domesday Book records twenty-eight burgesses within Lydford's walls, and forty-one without, so it was evidently a considerable and prosperous place, and that prosperity may have come from tin. It was, after all, well situated for trade, lying as it does between the two great highways of the moor: the Cornwall/Okehampton/Exeter road and the Okehampton/Plymouth road, with the old streamworks on Okehampton moor handy to them both. Later on Lydford was to become famous (and infamous) as the Stannary prison.

The first documentary references to tin production in Devon appear in the twelfth century. Though the lead and tin mines of England are included in the survey, Domesday Book makes no mention of Devon. But being a royal metal, tin was the property of the king, and this may account for the omission; for the main purpose of the Domesday Survey appears to have been an evaluation of estates outside the royal demesne with a view to taxation. The Normans and Angevin kings were probably the first to recognise tin as a potential source of royal revenue, and they may well have set to work building up an industry that already existed, though on a small scale.

The first brief recordings of the Devon Stannaries are entries in the Pipe Rolls. At this time, tin production seems to have been confined to Devon, for the revenue from the mines was entrusted to the Sheriff of Devon who in 1156 was paying £16.13s.4d per year into the Exchequer 'on account of the new farm',* and this was raised at frequent intervals to keep pace with the increase in production. The 'farm' was taken over in 1167 by a syndicate of three partners, William Baten, Alan Furneaux and Joel of Ashburton.

In the same year comes proof of a flourishing industry, when there was an increase in taxation, and in 1197 the Crown made a profit of £352.6s.10d on the purchase and resale of tin. The supervisor at this time was Geoffrey Fitz Peters, who held the manor of Lydford with all Dartmoor at farm, and was Justice of the Forest. It was however, becoming obvious that such a profitable industry needed the maximum supervision and encouragement, so in 1198 Geoffrey handed over his responsibilities to the second Warden of the Stannaries, William de Wrotham.

An early nineteenth century engraving portrays something of the grim aspect of Lydford Castle with its 'noisome dungeon'. Above: The two sides of a Lydford Penny produced in the mint that operated continuously for 100 years from the reigns of Æthelred II to Edward the Confessor. Though a handful of coins are held in museums in England, several hundred are in Scandinavian museums, no doubt once part of 'Danegeld'.

*'Farm' in this context refers to a fixed sum, usually paid annually, for the right to collect all revenue from land; in effect, rent. Many sheriffs farmed out their shires, contracting in advance to pay a fixed annual sum to the crown.

William got busy at once. One of his first acts was to assemble a jury of tinners in the County Court at Exeter, and by their testimony, establish the facts concerning duty paid on tin at the first smelting, and the system of weighing tin of the second smelting. The names of these tinners are interesting for they include men from Totnes, Plympton, Ashburton and Tavistock. (Did Roger Rubi or Rubbi belong to the family which gave its name to Rubby Town in Tavistock?). The changes resulting from this inquiry dealt mainly with taxation, de Wrotham's letter of 1198 records the reforms proposed for the government of the Stannaries. No one might retain possession of tin for more than a fortnight after the smelting unless it had been weighed in the presence of three Stannary officials who stamped it with the royal sign that duty had been paid. Within thirteen weeks thereafter all tin was to be put into a second smelting, and again weighed and stamped. These operations were to be performed at Exeter or Bodmin and a number of market towns designated from year to year by the Warden. At the second smelting the tin became liable to a new duty of one mark per thousand weight. Stringent rules were laid down to prevent evasion of payment.

The Exeter weight for tin of the first smelting is interesting for the pound used for this operation was eighteen Exeter ounces. This was to compensate for value, less foreign matter lost in the first smelting, the loss of value due to the tax of thirty pence per thousand weight, and the cost of transport to the town of the second smelting, where it was weighed and stamped. The price of the first smelting had to be lower than that of the second smelting.

A sharp rise in production followed this new legislation and the Crown quadrupled its revenue from the new duty, and from the tax on 'black tin'. But the industry was always fluctuating and production fell again around 1200. King John issued the first Charter of the Stannaries, a landmark in the history of the Stannaries of Devon, which was destined to set the medieval tinner apart from his fellows as a privileged person and potential source of disruption in the society of Dartmoor. The Charter confirmed the ancient privileges 'of digging tin and turfs, for smelting it at all times freely, peaceably and without hindrance from any man everywhere in the moors, and in the fees of Bishops, Abbots and Counts, and of buying faggots to smelt the tin without waste of forest and of diverting streams for their works in the Stannaries as by ancient usage they are wont to do.'

The first clause confirms the laws of bondage common to all mining communities, confirmation of this privilege made the tinner a free member of society, but even more important, by the second clause, he found himself removed from pleas of villeins so that only the Warden of the Stannaries had jurisdiction over him.

> *'We have granted that the Chief Warden of the Stannaries and the Bailiff through him, have over aforesaid tinners plenary powers to do them justice and hold them to law and that they be received by them to our prisons, if it shall happen that any of the aforesaid ought to be seized or imprisoned for the law, and if it shall happen that one of them be a fugitive or an outlaw to be through the hands of the Warden of our Stannaries, for the tinners are of our farm, and always in our demesne.'*

King John.

This Charter was most unpopular with the landlords, for it meant that a serf who wished to engage in stream tinning was exempt from pursuit by his lord, and free to set up his bounds anywhere in Devon. In 1204, King John disafforested Devon, possibly to give some compensation to these landlords, but he excluded Dartmoor which was, of course, the area where most of the county's tin was to be found.

Despite its unpopularity, the Charter was confirmed in the reigns of Henry III, and each of the three Edwards, and this was a subtle move on the part of the Crown for it gave encouragement to all men to seek the privileges of a tinner. When in 1203, the output of tin reached record levels, King John found himself amply justified.

During the thirteenth century there was little change in the administration of the Stannaries. In 1225, the King resumed farming his tin revenues thus removing them from the subjects in the Pipe Rolls and other state documents. From 1225 to 1300 the Devon and Cornwall Stannaries were under the jurisdiction, first for Richard and then Edward, Earls of Cornwall, but they left no records of ordinances or charters. Occasionally, when a lease expired and some time elapsed before the issue of a new one, there is an indication in the Pipe Roll of how the Stannaries were managed. For example, in 1243, the Devon Stannaries accounted to the King, and the Pipe Roll entries show that changes occurred in fiscal arrangements. The ancient 'farm' ceases, and 'black rent' is mentioned for the first time. This tax of two pence per head was paid by the digger of tin ore, and it provides a useful clue as to how many tinners were actually working in Devon until 1301 after which it disappears. From 1288 'white rent' is levied on those bringing ore to be smelted, and taking away the finished product.

The introduction of 'blowing houses' to Devon was a landmark, for so improved were the methods of smelting that a second refining process became unnecessary. The blowing houses evidently came to the moor between the date of King John's Charter (1201) and 1286, when the Pipe Roll entries for Devon are resumed, for by this time the new tax of 'white rent' had been imposed, and the stamp duties on tin of the first and second smeltings were consolidated into a single charge, permanently adopted in 1301 and known henceforth as coinage duty.

Towards the close of the thirteenth century there was once again an over-all drop in the tin production of Devon. This may have been due to heavy taxation by Richard of Cornwall (see chapter on Ashburton), but it may also be connected with the banishment of the Jews in 1198, temporarily ending their involvement in the tin industry. In 1305 another Charter was granted to the tinners of Devon. Edward I, taking full advantage of technological advances, used them as an excuse to boost production and increase his revenue. His Charter marked an important step in Stannary government, for in it were new features that further accentuated the differentials between the tinners and the rest of the community. But most significantly, it remained, except for one amendment, until the nineteenth century, as the effective constitution of the Stannaries. In brief, it confirmed the customary right of bounding, freed the tinners from ordinary taxation, confirmed the existing tin coinage and presumption of coined tin, by the Crown, and attempted to give precision to jurisdiction of the Warden and his lieutenants.

The coinage was held annually at Michaelmas in each of the Stannary towns, Ashburton, Chagford, Tavistock, and later Plympton. But if the tinners were prevented, by flooding or lack of water for washing, from presenting their tin at the regular coinages, post-coinages were held, and an additional duty of four pence per hundredweight was laid upon the tin. This is Lewis's reconstruction of proceedings at a coinage:

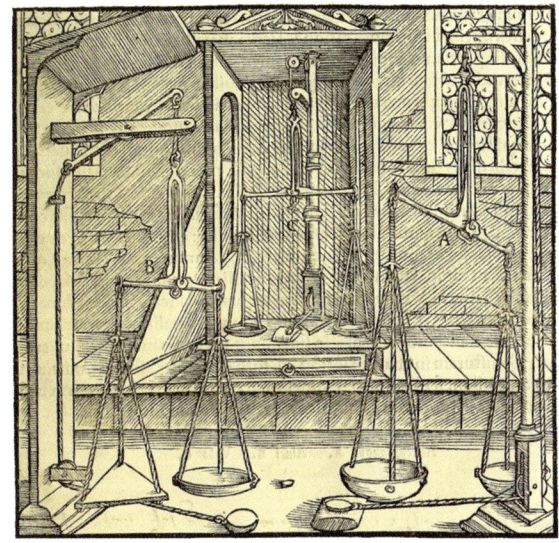

Weights and measures used by the officials appointed to value smelted metal. From De re metallica *by Georgius Agricola (Georg Bauer), a pioneering work on mining published in 1556.*

An open space was roped off in front and the King's beam brought out and rectified by controller and weigher. The weights were solemnly presented unsealed and handed to the weigher. The assay master made ready his hammer and chisels and the steward, controller and receiver took their seats facing the beam. Then the partners brought out the blocks of tin, one at a time, and placed them upon the scales. Each had been stamped with the private mark of the owner, and as the steward carried with him a register of these marks, there was no difficulty in identification. The weight of each was shouted out by the weigher and taken down by the three officials. The blocks on leaving the scales were taken in hand by the assay master who chiseled a small piece from a corner of each and rapidly assayed it to make sure that the metal was of proper quality. If so, the controller. with a blow of his hammer, struck upon the block the Duchy arms, but, should it be below standard, it was 'tared' by the assay master, that is to say, a relative figure was placed by him upon each block at which it might be sold below the market price for tin of standard quality. Having been stamped and weighed, it was returned to the coinage hall and a bill made out by the clerks for each tin owner. Setting for the number of his blocks, their weights, their firmness whether 'soft' or 'hard', and finally, the amount of coinage due upon the whole. When this had been paid the tin could be sold.

The elaborate procedure that surrounded the coinage emphasizes how important an item coinage duties were to the country's economy, at a time when the Crown was constantly in debt.

The Charter of 1305 was a potential source of disruption. Henry III's confirmatory Charter of 1252 had declared the Stannaries throughout Devon and Cornwall to be a royal demesne, and had forbidden any lord to 'implead'(prosecute) a working tinner as his serf. Edward I in 1305 limited this freedom to tinners 'working in these Stannaries which are in our demesne' and left it to become a matter of fierce dispute whether a tinner working elsewhere than on Crown land was entitled to the same protection. Another clause exempting working tinners from 'all tallages, tolls, stallages and aids, and all other customary dues in ports, fairs and markets within Devon', was construed by tinners as exempting them from national taxation. The Abbot of Tavistock who gained some of his income from the industry, was their spokesman on one occasion. Their bargaining power is well illustrated by events during Edward III's French Wars when the tinners, who refused to pay taxes of one fifteenth went on strike. In the end the Crown was forced to give in, and thereafter their right of exemption was absolute. But, perhaps the greatest cause of dissension was the actual definition of the privileged title of 'tinner'.

The Charters of 1201 and 1305 were addressed to 'all tinners so long as they are at work', but during the fourteenth century, a great many other people besides the actual diggers of tin claimed their privileges. So many complaints were raised against such persons that the Government in 1316 gave an official reply, defining the term 'tinner', 'as the normal workers in the tin mines so long only as they worked there'.

In Devon the existence of 'white rent' levied on the owners of 'white tin' seems to imply that there was a broad interpretation of the term, and the Charter of 1316 left the way open to dispute by dealing merely with special privileges granted to tinners on royal estates. After 1316 the flood of complaints steadily increased until in the Charter of Pardon 1507, the definition of who was, or was not a tinner had once and for all to be reviewed and interpreted. This time it included gentlemen bounders, owners of tin works, possessors of blowing houses' and buyers of 'black' and 'white tin'.

As we shall see later, this independent and contentious set-up had its own jurisdiction, operated by certain laws, customary and statutory, technical and non-technical for which the Warden was responsible. At the head of the Stannary system was the King, or from 1337, the Prince of Wales as Duke of Cornwall. Beneath him were the Warden and the lower statutory courts with their stewards and juries of miners. The Stannary Courts offered formidable competition to the Manorial Courts, for they dealt not only with tin mining offences, but adjudicated upon pleas of every description in which a tinner was either plaintiff or defendant. Their courts were of 'quyke spede', and their verdicts backed by the terror of Lydford dungeons.

Tavistock Abbey from a print by Samuel and Nathaniel Buck, 1734. The Abbey was among the first places in the country to establish a printing press following its introduction by William Caxton in 1476. It was here the earliest printed copy of the Stannary laws was made (see Appendices).

As with Manorial Courts the Stannary held a Customary Court and a Great Court. Of the Customary Courts, Carew writes: 'The tin of the whole shire came, and each is assigned by a land warden or steward who keeps a court called a Stannary Court which holds pleas of whatsoever action of debt or trespass where to by dealing with "black tin" or "white tin", either as defendant or plaintiff in a party.'

The *White Book* of Cornwall in an entry for March 11th, 1360 shows how valuable to the Prince of Wales were the fines paid by the tinners at the courts. In this document he orders that the fines be delivered to the keeper of the King's Stannaries, so that they may be available for the King's immediate use.

Where they exist the rolls of the Stannary Courts give an insight into the lives of the tinners, and among them are those of Tavistock. The Great Courts expanded into the Stannary Parliaments first recorded in 1494, though they had possibly been in existence for two hundred years. They chose Crockern Tor as their place of meeting, probably because it is equidistant from the four Stannary towns, and here tinners from all over Devon, seated on stone 'benches' around a granite 'table' and exposed to all weathers, discussed and enacted the laws of the Stannary.

Following the Charter of 1305 there was a fresh surge of mining activity lasting till the Black Death in 1348. There follows two apparently conflicting pieces of information about the industry. In 1354 the Close Rolls record an attack on a ship laden with Devon Stannary tin to the value of £250.16s.8d. But in the following year the coinage duty yield was nil. No doubt factors other than the

Few places on Dartmoor have excited so much controversy as Crockern Tor, its links with the Stannary and, in particular, the configuration of the so-called benches, table and the President's or Judge's Chair, some further details of which are discussed in the following chapter. This 1826 engraving is by P.H. Rogers.

plague were responsible for the fall in expenditure, which dates from before the Black Death. The French Wars, and later the Wars of the Roses encouraged smuggling and piracy, and the rising cost of labour and increased production of the German tin mines did much harm to the Stannaries of South West England. Throughout the period under review, we are constantly reminded of how vulnerable the tin industry was to violent fluctuation, and the same is true in Germany where the cause was said to be 'the capricious nature in revealing the ore, especially stream tin'.

By comparing the coinage dues from each of the Stannary towns we can see the movement westward of the productive areas of Dartmoor. For, as the stream tin of one of the river basins was used up, there was an interval before the next area to be exploited reached maximum production. The evidence of the fifteenth and sixteenth centuries suggests that streamworks became exhausted. So extensively had they been worked that the enormous quantity of gravel washed down the rivers were silting up their beds and choking harbours. Productive tin lodes are few in Devon, and the practice of shaft mining was not able to replace streaming until it was organised as a large-scale enterprise. Renewed activity does not occur again till the seventeenth century when improved techniques and organisation were introduced. So the end of the Middle Ages sees the end of the first era of tin mining on Dartmoor.

TRADE AND TRADE ROUTES

Tin has been a prized and sought-after metal since prehistoric times, for though its uses are many, its occurrence is rare. We have already seen that modern techniques allow for the origin of mined metals to be located to within a few miles of where they were dug from the ground. This helps support scanty documentary evidence that trade in tin from Devon and Cornwall dates back to the Bronze Age. Along with its importance in forming bronze when mixed with copper, tin was a vital ingredient in creating dyed cloth known as Tyrian purple or Phoenician red, the colour of royalty in ancient times, dating back at least 3000 years.

During the Middle Ages tin was made into solder bars with lead, and these became the principal stock-in-trade of travelling tinkers. It was also used for bell casting, and the accounts of Exeter Cathedral record the founding of two bells, the tin from which they were made being bought from William Ryka of Ashburton. Another use was decorative, for tin metal was made into bracelets, brooches, beads and costume jewellery. It was a handy counterfeit for silver and gold, retaining its lustre indefinitely, unlike silver which tarnishes with age and exposure. Monks mixed it with saffron to simulate gold in their manuscripts, and even the coffins of the royal and famous were fashioned from tin.

Being used in the preparation of dyes, tin had a connection with the wool trade too, but most of all it was required for pewter from which the majority of domestic articles of the medieval period were made. London and Bristol were the main centres for the manufacture of pewter and so were major ports to which tin was shipped.

Tin Streaming

In their *History of Cornwall* in 1824, Hitchens and Drew describe how the early tinners knew where best to seek out the ore that lay in the courses of rivers and streams, washed down from the main lode and deposited over centuries.

> As the tin ore on its discovery, must have been instantly found to be much heavier than any of the surrounding strata, those persons who first turned their attention towards it, would almost instinctively be led to examine the ground beneath the surface on which it appeared. And on finding a continuance of the ore until they discovered it resting on the solid rock, they would easily proceed to trace it through those vales in which the floods and torrents passed... It is this distribution of tin as deposited in Tallies, that constitutes what is generally called a stream work... But besides a stream of tin ground thus distributed through the valley, a stream of water is always necessary to separate the ore from the surrounding rubbish...

And so, making use of the streams, the tinners made their way along the valleys, digging down to reveal the layers of alluvial tin, separating the ore in sluices and piling the waste rock behind them as they went, often building revetments to hold back the heaps of soil and rock. It is the remains of these parallel banks of spoil that can still be seen on the moor today.

The remains of tin streaming on the valley floor west of Middle Staple Tor in tributaries of the River Walkham.

The methods of winning the tin ore from the stream bed varied widely, as did the means by which the ore was separated from the spoil. In the sketch opposite we see the water being diverted through the workings along wooden troughs or launders into which the ore-bearing deposits are shovelled by the miners. Here it is washed into sluices or tanks where the heavier tin ore can settle and be retrieved. The waste is then thrown back, behind revetted walls. Today these leave telltale ribs upstanding along the valley floors on the moor, as in the photo on the left.

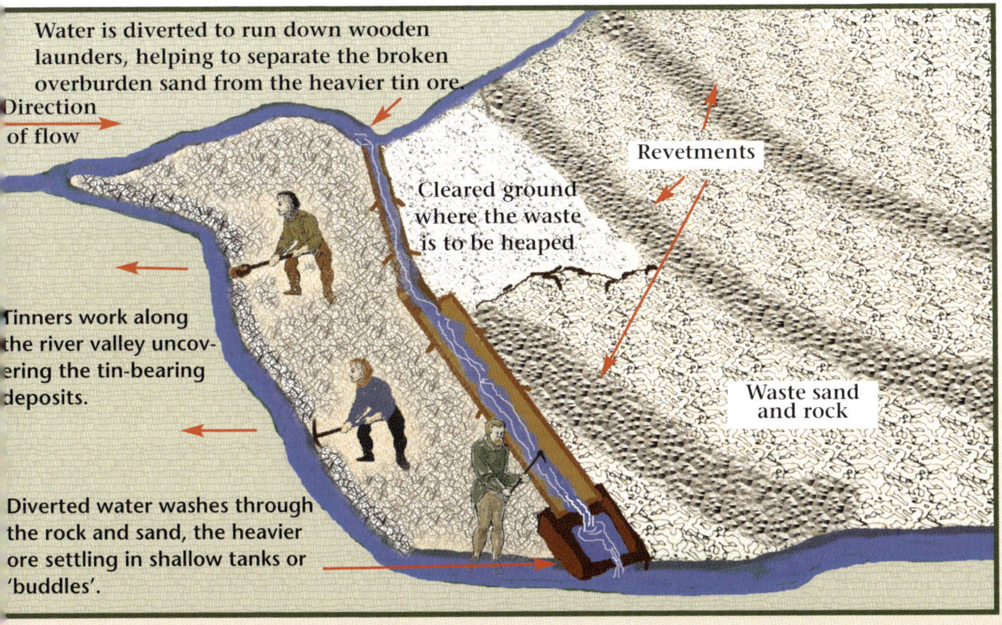

Water is diverted to run down wooden launders, helping to separate the broken overburden sand from the heavier tin ore.

Direction of flow

Revetments

Cleared ground where the waste is to be heaped

Waste sand and rock

Tinners work along the river valley uncovering the tin-bearing deposits.

Diverted water washes through the rock and sand, the heavier ore settling in shallow tanks or 'buddles'.

A number of early writers describe the method by which tin ore was won from stream beds including Bauer in De re metallica, *Hitchens and Drew in their* History of Cornwall, *and William Pryce in* Mineralogia Cornubiensis, *and much evidence remains on the moor to substantiate how this was done. The sketch above is based on the illustration in Phil Newman's* The Dartmoor Tin Industry: A Field Guide, *1998.*

Below: A tinner's cache at Headon, close to the Wallabrook. These were used by miners to store equipment and are usually found close to their workings.

Above: A revetted bank in the foreground reveals the work of tin streamers with the line of workings which can be seen receding along the valley floor beyond.

Another of the principal users was of course, the Crown. In 1195 more than 254 thousand-weight of Dartmoor tin was despatched to La Rochelle to adulterate the coinage with which Richard Coeur de Lion paid his troops, and in 1247 Henry III appealed urgently to the Sheriff of Devon that he should buy 4000 pounds of tin in his bailiwick and carry it to the King's works at Westminster. Most valuable was the right of preemption to the Crown which constituted a virtual monopoly often pledged to foreign merchants as security of loans. This right was the cause of many a complaint from the tinners. It was quite common for the King to send out such orders as: 'To the Merchants of the Society of the Bardi, by reason of letters patent appointing them to take all the tin of Devon and Cornwall for their use, as the King wishes to show favour to the merchants'.

King Henry II.

COMMUNICATIONS

Each of the Stannary towns had their major ports, from whence the coined tin was shipped. Recent excavations near Tavistock have revealed the remains of a medieval harbour and quay at Morwellham, and from here the tin probably went by river to Plymouth. Plympton tin was shipped down the Plym. Ashburton sent its product overland to Plymouth or, possibly, via Totnes, down river, to Dartmouth. Chagford's metal must have been carried to the waterfront at Exeter. The main tin shipping ports of Devon are listed in the Close Rolls of 1341 as 'Exeter, Topsham, Kenton, Teignmouth, Seaton, Sidmouth, Dartmouth, Brixham, Paignton, Kingsweare, Totnes, Portsmouth, Kings bridge, 'Yelem(ne)', Plymouth, Barnstaple and Bideford'.

Tin was shipped and traded in large amounts over long distances. During the twelfth and thirteenth centuries close relations were maintained between England and Germany through the tin trade until the German states were able to draw on their own market.

During the fourteenth century Bruges was the tin capital of Europe. In 1347 the Black Prince ordered the Bailiffs of Dartmouth to allow his merchant Tideman de Lynberg, to buy tin in his name and have it carried to Flanders. Wool and tin were transported direct to Italy and merchants from Genoa, Florence and Venice traded tin from the fourteenth century onwards. So, fostered by the protection of the Crown, the Dartmoor tin industry was able to play a part of international importance within the Stannary of South West England.

Chapter 2
Crockern Tor: The Stannary Parliament

The Dartmoor Tinners were a law unto themselves. From what we can surmise from the records, they were supreme individualists, interested in little beyond their work and their lodes. Tin was their life, and the Stannary their orbit. Small wonder that they quarrelled incessantly with their neighbours.

The Court Rolls of many a Devon manor and hundred record a stream of com-plaints against the tinners: they had dug into and destroyed tilled fields, woods, and gardens; they had silted up rivers; they had assaulted innocent persons, car-rying them into the Stannary, where they had chastised and imprisoned them. The tinners replied with accusations that 'foreigners' (those outside the Stannary) had presumed on their rights and damaged their works; that 'Lords impeded them for pleas of serfs'. The tinners usually won their case. Tin was a royal metal and the Crown set a great store by its revenue. The tinners looked to the King and the King protected them.

Though we do not know exactly when mining in Devon and Cornwall first came under the jurisdiction of the Crown, it was evidently at an early date, for the Charter of 1198 gives evidence that the tinners had long been possessed of their rights and privileges. Laws of a stringent character relating to the Stannaries had been in operation from a remote period, and though their origins are not known they had probably evolved from rude enactments considered necessary by the ancient workers in the early days of tin mining.

In the famous Charter of 1305 Edward I decreed 'That all Tinners working in the Stannaries of our demesne so long as they work for the same Stannary be free and quiet from all pleas of villeinies and all pleas and plaints of our court and our heirs, etc.' This Charter freed the tinners from tolls and customs, made their deportation from the Stannary illegal, granted them the right to dig for tin, 'everywhere in our lands, moors and wastes in the aforesaid country', and also the right to use the waters and water courses. The Lord Warden and his officers were to hold all pleas between tinners and others of trespass and complaint within the Stannary, and free power of justice was invested in the Warden. He was also to have powers of arrest and imprisonment. If any tinner outside the Stannary fell foul of the law, half the jury was to be comprised of tinners, and if any tinner was convicted of a serious offence he was to be handed over to the Warden. This Charter shows, beyond question, what a highly favoured race the tinners were, and what an advantage it was to live under royal patronage.

Small wonder that in 1318, in an effort to limit the power of the Stannaries, at a time when larger tracts of Dartmoor were coming under cultivation, the county of Devon made a public complaint to the Crown, alleging trespass and assault, imprisonment by the King's and other bailiffs in the Stannary prison at

Lydford, exhortation and violence by the Stannary officers, general impoverishment of the people of the area, and armed prevention of those trying to attend the hundred courts.

The tinners replied that acts of violence had been committed against them, that their works had been broken down and their tin stolen. Standing shoulder to shoulder as favoured subjects of the King they prevailed, and so-continued in their kingdom within the kingdom, bound by their own laws, and answering to none but the Warden and his officers.

United as they were by complex partnerships, honesty between these parties was essential, and from their earliest days they had evolved rigid and binding rules which, as time went on, became laws. When they first began to assemble together to enact these laws, we do not know. In the beginning joined with the Cornish tinners, they met on Hingston Down, but by 1305, they had undoubtedly separated, for the first part of the Charter grants privileges to Cornwall, and the second to Devon, confirming them as separate entities. Nor do we know when and why they chose Crockern to be their meeting-place. Their first recorded Parliament took place in September 1494, but undoubtedly they had been gathering there for decades, possibly several hundred years before that date.

Little can teach us more about the tinners than a study of their Parliament, most significant of all their place of assembly. It would be difficult to imagine anywhere less similar to Westminster, or any other site associated with the word

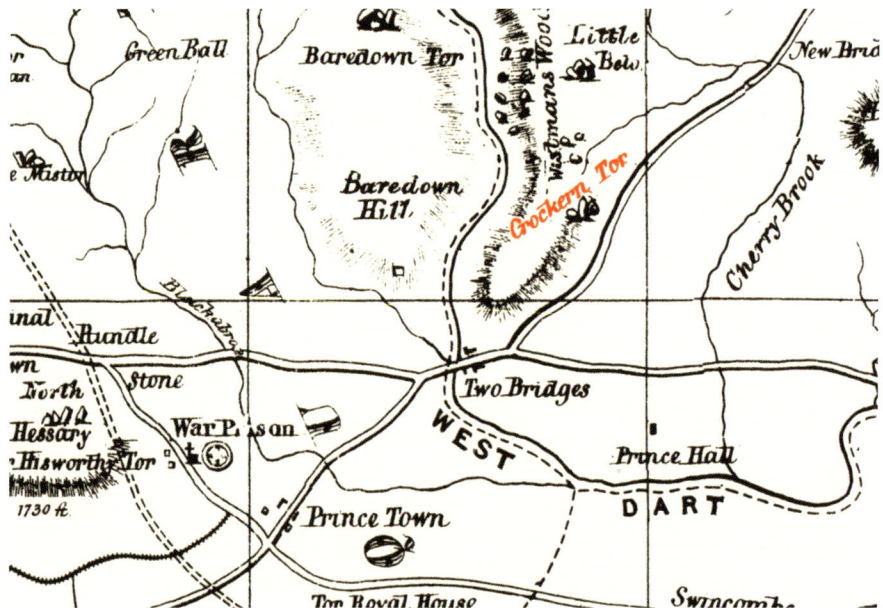

Detail from Samuel Rowe's map of Dartmoor first published in 1848, with Crockern Tor highlighted. Though seemingly remote, one can see from its proximity to settlements and trackways, why it would be a convenient site for the Stannary Parliament.

'Parliament'. They almost certainly chose Crockern because it is equidistant from the four Stannary towns and Lydford, and not, as the romantic Polwhele has it, because it was the site of an Ancient British Court. This pleasant grassy tor is reputedly the central point of the moor. The busy main road, which divides at Two Bridges, is less than a mile away from where hikers take the track from the car park which leads to Wistmans Wood. En route, half a mile away to their right, rises Crockern Tor with views across a wide moorland landscape.

It was very different in the days of the tinners, so we are told by early writers. On the summit of the tor, a great thin granite slab served as a table surrounded by stone seats, the Lord Warden's being surmounted by a stone canopy. Here on Parliament Days a large crowd assembled. Each Stannary appointed twenty-four jurats, ninety-six in all, in addition to the Lord Warden and officers, and, as many of these men had come on horseback, and would certainly need refreshment during the day, there must also have been a substantial company of 'extras', grooms, attendants, friends and relations, besides the inevitable locals who had 'come up to see the Parliament'.

Many of these people no doubt found accommodation in the neighbourhood for they had all come a considerable distance, and some from far afield. At one of the sixteenth century Parliaments, Chagford is unexpectedly represented by John Walcot of Chudleigh and John Bowden of Doccombe (between Moretonhampstead and Dunsford), Plympton by Thomas Ford of Brixham, and Tavistock by John Gee of Horrabridge.

One of the earliest photographs we have of Crockern Tor, taken by Robert Burnard in July 1890. He describes this as 'The Cyclopean Chair' and indeed the natural contour of the rock give it such an appearance.

Crockern Tor
Fact & Fancy

Dartmoor's landscape is perfect for the generation of myth and folklore, and in the history of tin mining Crockern Tor has provided many stories, particularly in relation to the Stannary Parliament. Antiquarians, suggest the place, as an assembly point, has roots in ancient times, going back to the Romans and possibly beyond. Its importance to tinners is well documented and, being more or less equidistant to the four Stannary towns and pitched where a number moorland roads come together, it would make perfect sense to hold meetings here.

It is in the more fanciful reporting by these early visitors of the 'furnishings' on offer to the Parliamentarians that controversy has occurred, with some painting a picture of purpose-made tables and seats, along with a Judge's Chair, hewn from granite. And it would only be natural for those following, on finding no such fixtures and fittings at the tor, to speculate on what might have happened to them.

Sure enough, with the 'discovery' of the 'seat' at Dunnabridge Pound (a prehistoric enclosure later in use as a pen for animals) and a large table-like stone covering a trough in the farmyard nearby, surely here was evidence enough to suggest these had been removed from the Tor to serve purposes elsewhere. From such speculation is folklore born.

For redoubtable Edwardian antiquarians, matters reached a head in correspondence in the *Western Mercury* in 1909 in which William Crossing provided a lengthy riposte, quoting early writers and local farmers, to the suggestion that either the Dunnabridge 'chair' or the farmyard table top were ever at the Tor. He is supported in this by Robert Burnard who photographed both structures and wrote that the belief either came from Crockern Tor 'very doubtful', although on his 1888 photo caption of the trough he repeats the story of the Stannary table.

Opposite from top: Crockern Tor from a watercolour by T.A. Falcon c.1900; The Judge's Chair at Dunnabridge Pound from an 1888 engraving; Burnard's 1892 photo of the Judge's Chair; The water trough at Dunnabridge Farm – its cover stone once purported to be the Stannary table from Crockern Tor. Above: John Swete's watercolour of the 'Trilithon in Dunnabridge Pound' which depiction supports the view it has prehistoric origins, while others (see the present-day photo below) have suggested it is a more recent construction, built as a shelter for those overseeing animals in the pound.

For centuries agriculture had flourished in this central basin of Dartmoor, and thirty-five farms known as the Ancient Tenements, had long been established. Nine of these farms are less than thirty minutes by pony from Crockern, which suggests that thanks to the Tinners' Parliament, the bed and breakfast trade must have been a going concern in this part of the moor hundreds of years before the twentieth century tourist boom.

At the groups of farms and tenements of Prince Hall, Bellever, Dunnabridge, Broom Park, Brownberry, Huccaby, Hexworthy and Sherberton, one might imagine a great brewing and baking, and airing of linen come Parliament time. For several days, perhaps the best part of a week, judging by the length of the agenda, these usually quiet places would be crowded with men and horses. The Parliament would have been a time of excitement, a break in the day-to-day round, and a welcome addition to their income.

Several ancient pack-horse routes converged in the Crockern area, that from Exeter and Chagford to Plymouth passing at the foot of the tor. At Two Bridges a pair of clappers spanned the Cowsic and West Dart just before their meeting, thus giving the place its name, and alongside these clappers were the ancient fords that had predated them. This way came the Tavistock men. Their road can still be traced between the tor and the two rivers, and again where it climbs towards Omen Beam and down to the Blackabrook, where they crossed by clapper near Fices Well. Westward this old track climbed the hill near Rundlestone, before descending to Merrivale ford and bridge on the Walkham. From here to Tavistock it followed the course of the present main road.

Many of the Chagford jurats would have taken the eastward continuation of this ancient road, which branches near the Warren House Inn (known in the eighteenth century as New House), one fork going to Moretonhampstead and Dunsford, and the other passing over Hurston Ridge and Willand Head to Chagford.

A portion of John Ogilby's 1675 road map showing the route from Chagford to Crockern Tor. The map, produced in the form of a continuous strip, shows the track the Chagford jurats would have taken, heading past Waye Barton and joining the modern B3212 above Lakeland, then on 'past a stone called Merry Pitt' and 'a stone bridge 3 arches called Post bridge', past 'Chirrey brooke' to 'a Hill of Rock calld Crokha Tor'.

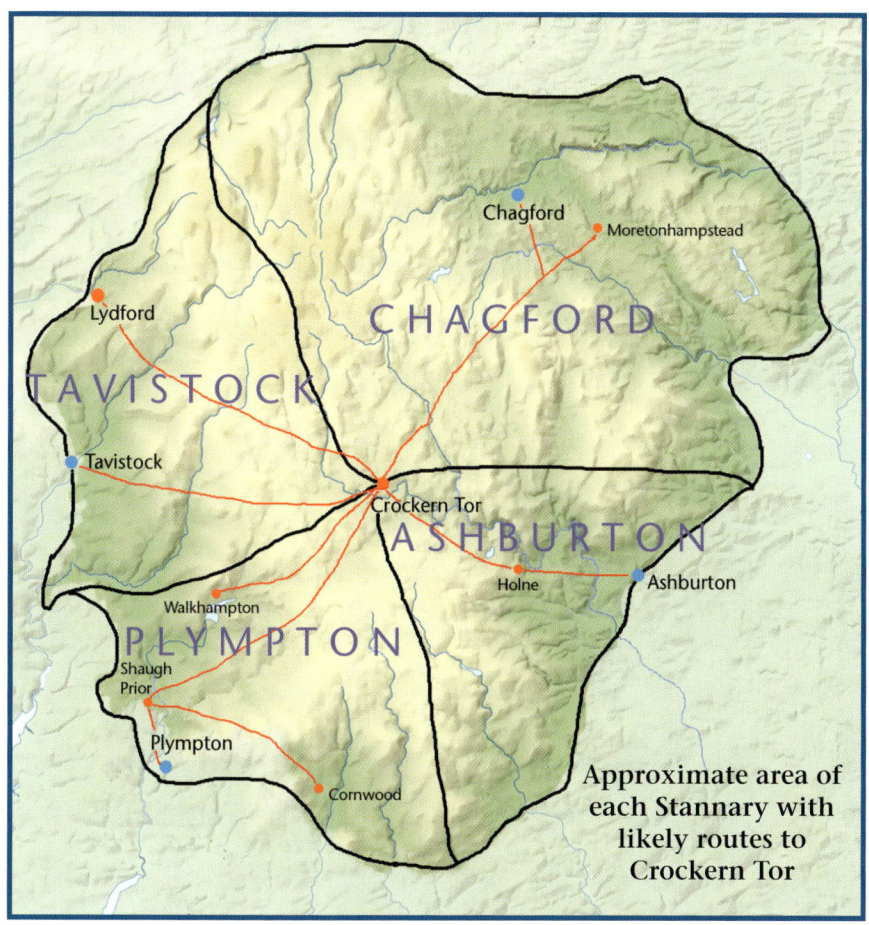

Approximate area of each Stannary with likely routes to Crockern Tor

From Ashburton they had a choice of route, for after they had gone through Holne and Hexworthy, they could either pass Swincombe Ford and Prince Hall, or they could go via Sherberton to cross the West Dart at Laughter Hole Steps steps and, skirting Dunnabridge, make straight for Smith Hill and Crockern.

The party from Plympton, and this included the men from Shaugh Prior and Sheepstor, probably rode towards Newlycombe Head, and so by Strane Ford and Roundhill to Two Bridges.

Finally, there was the Warden and his band. In 1494 he was Sir Philip Champernowne, and he had to ride twenty-five miles from Modbury to Crockern.

Let us suppose that the sun shone on their journey for, whichever way they came, they crossed splendid country, and in clear weather, would enjoy the finest views the moor has to offer. Had September 11th 1494 dawned fine and warm on Crockern as the jurats gathered for the Parliament, so the day would have started well. If it were wet, cold and foggy, as it often is up on the high moor, it might have been very unpleasant indeed for these sturdy parliamentarians, and dismal too for the Lord Warden and his officers who were not quite so used to being out on the moor in rain and mist as were the tinners.

A great Court held near Tavistock in 1571 having 'enacted rules for Bakers and Brewers for their court that there be no false measures' promptly adjourned to the town itself for the rest of their session. But that was not possible at remote Crockern in 1494, so we can assume that, at a respectful distance from the proceedings, carts and wagons containing ale and victuals were drawn up, booths erected, and no doubt, there was trading and amusement for the company. It must have been rather like the accompaniments of a point-to-point. As they gossiped and chatted, exchanging views of the outside world, as the ale flowed free, and children chased amongst the stunted oaks of Wistmans Wood, all the while from Crockern Tor came the hum of the Parliament, the slow Devon burr, now steady, now agitated, as some indignant jurat recounted outrages perpetrated by 'foreigners' from outside the Stannary.

Of the agendas left to us, the earliest is that of 1510, and as there is no great dissimilarity between it and a later survivor, we may conclude that many of the same problems were discussed in 1494, and at the Parliaments of former years.

The Lord Warden and his officers having taken their seats, the ninety-six jurats were sworn and satisfactorily shown to be approved by the whole body of Devon tinners. We know the names of the 1510 jurats, and these

J.W. Tucker's somewhat fanciful depiction of Crockern Tor. The artist has included a small stone hut in the lee of the tor.

are listed in the Appendix. A number of surnames are still familiar in the area today and may be of interest to family historians.

First they enacted that all former statutes be declared null and void, and that laws about to be passed be affirmed by the court. Thirty-seven enactments were recorded by the clerk. Some of these were merely formal, but others were undoubtedly controversial which suggests that the debates went on for some considerable time, probably several days. Meetings can be very wordy, and the tinners, who only got their chance once a Parliament, no doubt made the most of it. They began by discussing justice in, and outside, the Stannaries, firmly asserting their independence and insisting that all pleas except those concerning life, land and limb, be pleadable only before the Lord Warden and his court. This of course, involved the tin works themselves, the right to dig etc. and the use of water. The Warden's court was empowered to impose penalties, and fines upon the guilty parties.

Next they affirmed the coinage and stamping decrees. As these had not changed through the centuries they probably spent little time over them, but moved on to a set of much more debatable problems: the rights of the tinners themselves and actions that they might bring against each other. They probably argued about this for hours, taking up all the disagreements that had taken place since the last Parliament between themselves and sundry foreigners, arguing reasonable fines (£40, half to the informer and half to the court, etc.), commitments to Lydford and jury service in their Stannary.

Rights and titles to works and the employment of workers was the next item, and then they moved on to the marking of ingots, partnerships and the rights of minors and widows inheriting works.

Penalties were next imposed upon tinners refusing to pay fines, and laws were passed relating to 'washes', and the selling of uncoined tin, a serious offence. This involved more laws relating to the rights of partners re 'washing'.

Now came a number of enactments relating to 'wronged' tinners who, if they had not obtained justice from the Steward, could lay their case before the Under Warden, and if he did not give them satisfaction, before the Lord Warden himself and the Prince's Council (Duchy of Cornwall). They probably took a considerable time over this, and ended by fining the 'Sheriff, Bailiff or any person arresting or troubling a tinner at his work, £20' (half to the Prince and half to the Stannary), loyalty being absolutely essential to the tinners collective survival.

They also made certain that they might understand what was going on in their courts by insisting that every 'learned man' pleading in the courts of the four Stannaries, must do so in English. If he lapsed into Latin, or any other foreign tongue his plea would be null and void.

The final enactments, certainly of the middle and later Tudor Parliaments, and possibly that of 1494, dealt with a very important and controversial subject, the silting up of rivers and ports with sand from the streamworks. So furious did Dartmouth and Plymouth become over this perennial bone of contention, that a Tudor MP, Richard Strode, having introduced a Bill at Westminster restraining the tinners, found himself imprisoned at Lydford for three weeks. As soon as he was free, he petitioned Henry VIII and the Imperial Parliament that the highhanded judgement of the tinners be quashed, and though nothing was done for some years, the King finally recognised their responsibility, and a number of Acts were passed preventing gravel from being washed into the rivers.

In later Tudor Parliaments, also, there were decrees penalizing offenders who bought and sold tin illegally, and removed black tin unknown to the owners; those found guilty of bribery and corrupt evidence; and above all coiners of unstamped tin. Weights and measures too were confirmed by these sixteenth century jurats, and as the Elizabethan enclosures proceeded, laws relating to works in woods and cultivated ground, and water through private property.

But this was in the future, Lord Warden Champernowne, having been empowered to correct and amend statutes which needed it, the jurats, stiff and tired from their long sitting, rose at last from their stone seats, and hobbled off to the wagons for a jack of ale before the long ride home. September mists closed over Crockern, silent once more at the approach of winter. The excitement was over, and the Ancient Tenements returned to their daily round, shut away from the world till the next Parliament.

For hundreds of years the Stannary jurats tramped over the hills to Crockern. But the great days of tin were drawing to a close and the last Stannary Parliament probably sat in 1794. After that they came no more.

As has been discussed there is considerable discrepancy as to the fate of the Parliament's so-called table and chairs, or indeed if such 'furnishings' ever existed.

Risdon refers to them, and classes Crockern Tor as one of three most remarkable things on Dartmoor. But Wescote does not mention them. John Laskey avers in his article in the *Gentleman's Magazine* of 1795 that no chairs or table were to be seen on the tor when he went there, so he concluded that the jurats must have sat on the outcrop. But on making inquiries he was told that they had been removed to Prince Hall by the owner, Mr Gullett.

Prince Hall later became the residence of Sir Francis Buller, and both Carrington's *Dartmoor* (1826) and Worthy's *Ashburton* (1876) ascribe to him or rather his bailiff, Mr Leamon, the spoliation of Crockern. According to Worthy the stones were broken up and removed by workmen for building purposes unknown to Judge Buller. Carrington noted that the 'table', a thin granite slab, had been taken to Dunnabridge Farm as cover for a trough where potatoes were washed. In 1831 the Reverend E.A. Bray was told by the farmer at Dunnabridge that the slab in question had already been in place, to his knowledge, for fifty years.

Above: The potato trough at Dunnabridge Farm.

Sir Francis Buller, 1st Baronet, a judge and MP for Cornwall.

John Swete's watercolour of Prince Hall, Buller's home on Dartmoor, painted in 1797. Swete mentions the bridge as being recently built, each end mounted on 'immense blocks of granite'. Perhaps some of the stones his workmen are said to have taken from Crockern Tor?

As noted, the canopied stone in nearby Dunnabridge Pound which went by the name of the Judge's or President's Chair, was almost certainly not that of the Lord Warden, but the possible remains of a dolmen or cromlech made into a seat.

Rowe's *A Perambulation of the Forest of Dartmoor* appeared in 1835 and, during his researches, he records meeting an old man, formerly in the service of Judge Buller, who had lived on the moor for sixty years. He remembered 'perfectly well' when there was a chair or stone seat at Crockern 'with steps to go up to it, and overhead a large, flat thinnish stone'. These were all gradually taken away for building, the last about twenty years before that time. As this conflicts with Laskey, Crossing believes that the steps were a natural conformation, and that little beyond a large slab serving as a table, another projecting over the President's place, and stone lumps of granite used as seats, were all that were ever to be seen at Crockern. In more recent times, Jeremy Butler, in his *Dartmoor Atlas of Antiquities* (1991) also dismisses the idea of bespoke granite furnishings and suggests the tinners simply made use of the natural moorstone.

But whatever they were and wherever they went, they are gone, along with the Warden and the jurats, and the old proud days of the Parliament, when the tinners of the Royal Stannary snapped their fingers at the world at large, and made their laws to suit themselves in pursuit of the King's metal mined from the heart of the moor.

Chapter 3
Lydford: The Stannary Prison

From the Stannary Parliament to Lydford's Stannary prison – as grim and uninviting as HM Prison at Princetown is today. Visitors to Lydford today are rather more interested in the spectacular gorge or exploring the interior of the Castle Inn than the Castle itself, which still retains a somewhat forbidding air of menace.

The earliest origins of the settlement are cloaked in obscurity. The discovery of a shard of early pottery incorporated in the town's bank defences may point to a Dark Age settlement, possibly in the sixth century. The parish church is dedicated to that famous Celtic Saint, Petrock, who may well have extended his missionary activities to the banks of the Lyd, if he could find a congregation. Perhaps he came down the old highway from Isca to Cornwall. It was no distance from Lydford, and was an important route for sixth century merchants from overseas, trading in Cornish tin, who may possibly have been responsible for early prospecting on Dartmoor. Whatever Lydford's earliest history, by the ninth century it had become a burgh.

Lydford Gorge, which once held a perilous reputation, today draws thousands of tourists to the village each year.

When the Danes flung themselves against the southern shores of England, burning and plundering wherever they went, Alfred of Wessex set up a defence line along the borders of his kingdom, constructing a system of fortifications at strategic points. These were 'the burghs', and the ninth century list, known as the Burghal Hidage names Lydford among them.

Built in a position of great strength, it rose upon a promontory formed by a junction of the deep gorge of the Lyd on one side, and a steep sided valley on the other. It was planned to provide a ready company of men who could defend the walls against attack and (Lydford being one of the more elaborate burghs), who could bring their families into the stronghold. Saxon Lydford's streets were built to a neat grid system with shops available and a church for worship. Its principal entry is still used as a main road, and the systematic street pattern can dimly be traced through grass-grown lanes that cross the present highway at right angles.

When, thanks to the efforts of Alfred, and the strong rulers who followed him, the land (at least temporarily) had peace from the Northmen, Athelstan who became King early in the tenth century, did not forget the burghs. Under his rule they changed from fortresses to thriving commercial centres. Lydford soon had its own market and was minting its own coins. It served as one of the four Devon mints, and of equal importance with Exeter, Totnes and Barnstaple, a fact that seems almost unbelievable today. Standing in this sleepy little village it is well nigh impossible to imagine the bustling crowds, and the busy market of a thriving town whose wealth and reputation led to the tragedy of 997. For that year the Danes returned and the former burgh could defend itself no longer. Avid for plunder, they roared in, sacking the town and fortress. The terrified citizens, to prevent further damage, bought off their persecutors, Danegeld, that the sea rovers carried home in their longships.

Despite this misfortune, Lydford continued to prosper, so that by the Domesday Survey, it is described as a Royal Borough with, as has been stated, twenty-eight burgesses living within the town and forty-one without. Three of these, inhabitants are recorded as having come from Fernworthy, eight miles away.

All was not well, however, for with the coming of the Normans, Lydford's days as a trading centre were numbered, and the place was destined to gain a very different reputation.

Having stormed the town in 1068, the conquerors proceeded to throw up a castle on the south-west promontory. To do so they had to demolish forty houses, which fact gives us some idea of the size of Lydford before the Conquest. The original wood and earth structure was completed in 1088 and was destined to grow into the famous (and in the eyes of many, infamous) Stannary prison.

Lydford Castle and church c.1800.

For though by the early twelfth century, Lydford's importance as a military stronghold had been taken over by the large castles at Launceston and Okehampton, in 1195 a massive stone keep superseded the Norman fort. This was raised expressly for the custody of offenders against the Forest and Stannary Laws. To this day it stands, a majestic and sinister ruin, and a lasting reminder of the power and influence once vested in Lydford.

Why Lydford was chosen as the centre of Stannary administration is not known. The town probably had links with the tin trade in Saxon times, though there is no mention of this in the Domesday Survey, possibly because tin was a Crown metal and the Conqueror was more concerned with the possessions of his Knights than with his own. Certain it is that from the thirteenth century onward Alfred's burgh became the stronghold of the Stannaries.

Unfortunately for Lydford, as the stannators took over, the town slowly died. Traders ceased to ply their wares in those once busy streets, instead they turned their steps towards Tavistock and Okehampton, where expanding industries and rising populations promised better business. The Lydford burgesses tried to protect themselves by forming a merchant guild, but their royal overlord would have none of it, and fined them heavily for their pains. As compensation, however, the Crown, in 1197, did grant them an annual allowance 'for making Lydford market as it used to be of old'. Evidently it was not successful.

But though it was no longer a commercial centre, the moorland people still came to Lydford for spiritual care. For them it was a place of death, the goal of many a grim and tragic journey. As the parish church of the moor, it was to St Petrock's that the people of the Ancient Tenements on the lower land near the Wallabrook came to receive the sacraments and, at length, to bury their dead.

Even today the castle retains a sense of gloom and foreboding.

Lydford Castle

I oft have heard of Lydford Law
How in the morn they hang and draw,
And sit in judgement after...
William Browne 1644

In 1086, following the Conquest, William had a small defensive earthwork built close to the site of the present-day castle. It was King John, in 1194, who ordered the building of the castle we see today as a prison for those accused of crimes against Forest or Stannary Law.

The castle served as both a court room and a prison, the former likely to have been on an upper floor with rooms below serving as cells, perhaps offering varying degrees of discomfort, with a final dungeon, a pit, accessed by a trapdoor.

The gaol's most distinguished occupant was Richard Strode, MP for Plympton, whose attempts to stop the miners silting up rivers with their workings, saw him thrown into the 'deepe pitte' for three weeks.

In 1650 the castle was described as being almost totally in ruins but this didn't prevent the Royalists using it to hold prisoners during the English Civil War.

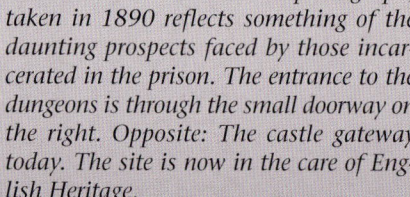

Above: Robert Burnard's photograph, taken in 1890 reflects something of the daunting prospects faced by those incarcerated in the prison. The entrance to the dungeons is through the small doorway on the right. Opposite: The castle gateway today. The site is now in the care of English Heritage.

The reason for establishing a mint at Lydford has been the subject of some debate but it is likely that, with the establishment of a defensive work by Alfred c.AD911, to combat raids by the Danes, the site would also serve to provide security for a mint.

Since Roman times, it was known that lead mines also produced silver and having such mines close to Lydford would give a convenient supply of metal for producing Lydford Pennies. It would also establish a close tie between the town, mining and miners. It has been estimated that 1.5 million coins were produce here until the mint ceased production c.AD1050.

Above: Robert Burnard's annotated 1883 OS map marking the position (in red) of the original Saxon defensive site, the wall and gateway protecting the burgh. The aerial photo, similarly marked, shows how close the site was to nearby Kitt lead mine from which silver was also extracted. Below: An etching of 1810 showing Lydford's castle and church. Inset: The obverse of the earliest known Lydford Penny, minted c.AD973 by the moneyer Ethelred and showing the head of King Edgar. This now forms the logo of the Dartmoor Trust.

This 1913 photo from the Taylor Collection in the Dartmoor Trust's Archive shows the ruinous state of Lydford Castle at that time. Such photos are imporant in understanding the changes that have taken place in the National Park's built environment.

Along the Lychway, across some of the wildest areas of the moor trailed the procession of mourners bearing the coffin, an eerie path on a winter's day, past the misty wraiths of Wistmans Wood and Beardown. As they trudged on, mile after mile, the tinners working on Willsworthy and Yellowmead streams might pause for a moment in respect. As the mourners gathered round the grave, high above them, sullen and sinister, rose the Norman castle keep, its reputation as sombre as its appearance. As administrative centre of the Stannary Forest Laws, it was here guilty wrongdoers found themselves tried and imprisoned. The name of Lydford had become a byword for harshness and tyranny.

We read in the previous chapter of the long suffering Devonians who petitioned Edward III to remedy the evils they were enduring at the hands of the tinners. Among many other injustices was the discrimination in how the law treated tinners and non-tinners. If a 'foreigner' should be unfortunate enough to transgress against the Old Men of the Moor, the chances were that the hold of Lydford would close upon him, and that was the last his friends would see of him, perhaps for ever. But despite these injustices, petitions to the Crown had little effect.

King Edward III.

The stannators were King's men, mining the King's ore, and they knew very well that whatever they did, their royal master would protect them. Lydford Keep was to them the symbol of their Warden and the dominion of the Stannary.

We know something of what the prisoners suffered from the mouth of Richard Strode, Member of Parliament for Plympton in the reign of Henry VIII. He had been bold (or foolish) enough to present a bill which would have restricted the silt pouring into the rivers from tin mines, and he was arraigned before the Stan-nary Court and clapped into Lydford for his pains. He describes himself as being 'imprisoned in a dungeon and a deepe pitte underground, the which prison,' he feelingly declared, 'is one of the most obnoxious, contagious and detestable places within this realm'. To avoid being put in irons and fed on nothing but bread and water, he had to pay his keeper one mark, with the promise of more. Being a man of substance, Strode soon obtained his freedom. Others were not so fortunate, nor had they the money with which to pay off their gaolers.

Just over a hundred years after Strode languished in Lydford, the castle had had its day, and in 1650 it was described as being in a ruinous condition. The power of the Stannary was broken, and offending foreigners would be summoned no more to Lydford. Yet such was its reputation in the years of tyranny, that a web of superstition and evil had been cast about its hollow shell. Judge Jeffries, in the form of a pig, and the black dog of wicked Lady Howard are said to lurk in the shadow of the keep.

Certainly this sinister relic of the Middle Ages does seem a little out of place in a sleepy old village, and tourists much prefer the waterfall and the gorge. But even here there is a pool called the Devil's Cauldron!

Even in relatively modern times the castle retains an air of melancholy and menace, as in this Robert Burnard photograph taken in March 1890.

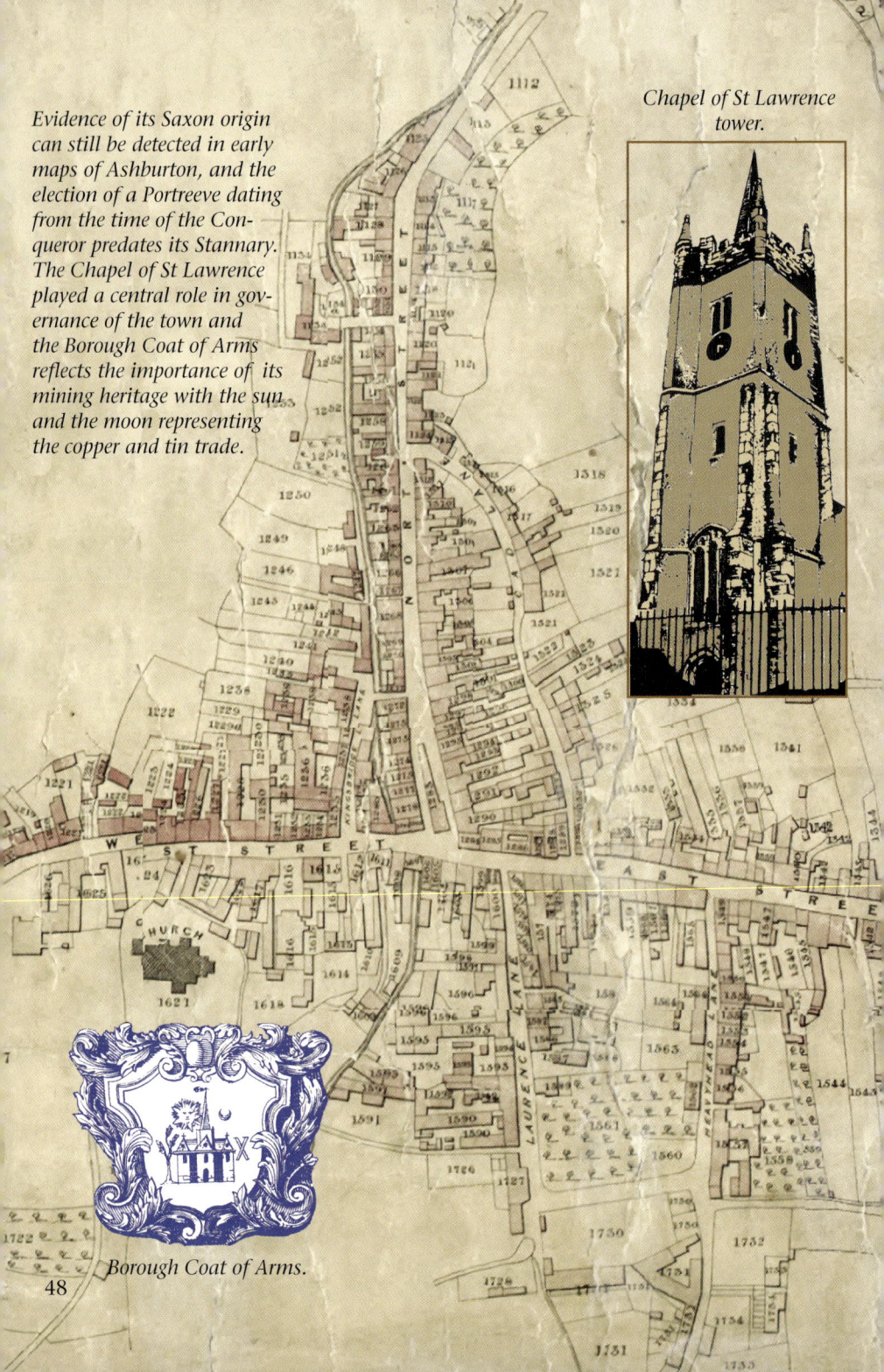

Evidence of its Saxon origin can still be detected in early maps of Ashburton, and the election of a Portreeve dating from the time of the Conqueror predates its Stannary. The Chapel of St Lawrence played a central role in governance of the town and the Borough Coat of Arms reflects the importance of its mining heritage with the sun and the moon representing the copper and tin trade.

Chapel of St Lawrence tower.

Borough Coat of Arms.

48

Chapter 4
Ashburton: The Royal Manor

A town with 'an air of respectable antiquity', such was the impression of the writer on Ashburton in *The Book of Fair Devon* in 1901, and it is still true of the place today. To all intents and purposes this is a nineteenth century town, for after a disastrous fire in the early 1800s it was largely rebuilt. In 1876 Charles Worthy recorded: 'The town consists of a long street traversing it from east to west, and two others leading north and south. The first three are filled with good houses and shops and the last terminated by the railway station.'

This description still holds good except for the station. The last train puffed away in 1971. Though the eastern end of the town straggles away in a grey development of housing estates, the west end is largely unchanged. Comfortable Victorian houses and gardens behind high walls drift down the hill to 'The Gateway of the Moor', the road which, branching, leads to two of the most beautiful of the Dartmoor villages, Holne and Buckland, then on and up to Widecombe and Postbridge, the same road, down which the tinners came to the Stannary Coinage. For this is a town which has a past which has even touched the fringes of European history, a past that is still in evidence.

Ashburton has a Portreeve and Bailiff, a Court Leet and Baron Jury. The Portreeve, whose title derives from 'portus' a trading centre and the Saxon office 'gerefa', now written 'reeve', originated in 920 under King Edward the Elder. The Portreeve authenticated transactions of all kinds of property and assisted in many administrative matters. Under Athelstan in 925, he organised public charity, a duty he still performs today. After the Norman Conquest the borough obtained the right to elect its Portreeve and there has been a continuous line of them ever since. The first whose name is known for certain was Robert Michel in 1335. The Portreeve played an important part in the affairs of the Stannary.

The Court Leet which, with the Court Baron, has met for the last 600 years in Old St Lawrence Chapel, was, and is, composed of elected freeholders of the borough and still has the power to make public 'presentiments' on matters of general interest. It elects the Portreeve and his assistant, the Bailiff of the borough, together with Ale Tasters and Bread Weighers. At the annual meeting the roll for a View of Frankpledge, whereby the Saxons ensured communal responsibility, is submitted before the elections and the making of presentiments.

The Court Baron, which once dealt with affairs of the manor, now elects Viewers of the Market (Inspectors), Viewers of Watercourses, Scavengers and Pig Drovers. These Offices, so necessary in their day, are now sinecures with one exception, the Ale Tasters. In the Middle Ages, Church Ale was brewed in the old Church House in North Street, the vessel used being sometimes referred to as a 'chetell' sometimes as a 'cacubus' (Latin for cauldron).

49

The two young men chosen as Ale Wardens having made a collection among the parishioners and employed the contributions towards the brewing, met with their neighbours in the Church House at Whitsuntide. Here, having feasted on their own victuals, the Wardens laid statement of their accounts before the parishioners, and the money in hand was devoted to defraying any extraordinary expenses, such as the repair of bells, towers, churches and the needs of the poor. These days their successors, the Ale Tasters, make a tour of licensed premises one evening during the Summer Carnival Week and carry out the ceremony of Ale Tasting as part of the activities in aid of local charities. This custom goes back possibly to the old Saxon 'Drink Pean', a day of festivity formerly observed by the tenants and vassals of the Lord of Fee within his manor.

Indeed Aysheberton (sometimes spelt Aistern and Asperton), the town on the Ashburn (now the river Yeo) was probably a settlement in Roman times as coins of Claudius, Decius and other Roman Emperors, and specimens of Romano British pottery have been found in the vicinity. The relative proximity of Isca, Dumnoniorum (Exeter) would explain this connection with the Empire. Ashburton too was on the 'Path of St Petroc', the probable founder of the first religious settlement at Buckfast in the sixth century. The earliest surviving document which actually refers to the neighbourhood of Ashburton goes back to the first half of the eleventh century and is in connection with a perambulation 'at the Ashburn outfall on Dart's stream to the Webburn outfall'.

During the reign of Edward the Confessor, the Manor was held by Britric, a wealthy and influential Thane, who so the story goes, was sent by the King on a mission to Baldwin, Count of Flanders. The Count's daughter, Matilda, was so charmed by him that she suggested marriage. But Britric took fright and returned to Devon, and perhaps also to his real love, for not long after, he married Godeva, heiress of Torre (now Torbryan).

Buckfast Abbey ruins from a print by Samuel and Nathaniel Buck, 1734. Prior to the Dissolution the Abbey had long enjoyed links with Ashburton, particularly through the wool trade. Inset: St Petroc.

Unfortunately, Matilda had not finished with Britric. She married William, Duke of Normandy, and, after the Conquest, she revenged her former humiliation, by appropriating Britric's lands, though not Godeva's, and the luckless Thane, taken at his Manor of Hanley, died in prison at Winchester. ('Doubtful evidence,' says King in his *Dartmoor Forest and its Borders*, 'but it is certain that eighteen Manors in Devon, among which are Ashburton and Bideford, are recorded in the Domesday Survey as having passed from the hands of Britric into those of the Queen.').

According to the Exchequer Domesday, Britric paid geld for three hides. The Royal Manor as it now became, consisted of ten carucates of land, and in the demesne were two carucates, four serfs, and seven villeins. There were eight borders with three carucates, two fisheries and one salt pit; three acres of meadow, and forty acres of pasture. Woodland, one league in length and half a league in breadth, rendered £4.

The famous Judhel de Totenais received the manor from Queen Matilda and held it till he fell foul of William Rufus who banished him and, rather surprisingly, gave it to the Bishops of Exeter. They continued to hold it, as part of their barony from the King in chief, by finding two soldiers for service in the royal army, until 1608 when James I resumed full royal rights.

So Church and State became the key factors in the history and development of Ashburton; tin, the royal metal, and wool fostered by the farmer monks, Richard of Cornwall and Bishop Stapledon, so the pattern continues throughout the Middle Ages.

The existence of various tin lodes on the Ashburn prompted the activities of the early settlers, and the discovery of Roman coins in walls, foundations and wells may point to a place of exchange between tinners and merchants.

Snow on the clapper over the Ashburn – it was by this route that miners would have approached Ashburton from the higher moor.

The Blowing House

There are literally hundreds of ruined buildings to be found on the moor, some now just a jumble of stones, others more clearly defined as to their original purpose. Those associated with mining have been described generically as 'blowing houses' although the blowing house itself had a specific purpose, as did the stamping mill or 'knacking house'. There would be some variation in what went on inside these, often hastily constructed, buildings, but the principal purpose of the blowing house was in smelting the ore in a furnace and producing ingots of tin, the raw tinstone having first been crushed in the stamping mill. Celia Fiennes on her travels through the Westcountry in 1699 describes the process:

> Half a mile from thence they blow their tin, which I went to see. They take the ore and pound it in a stamping mill which resembles the paper mills, and when it is as fine as the finest sand, this they fling into a furnace and with it coal to make the fire. So it burns together and makes a violent heat and fierce flame; the metal by the fire being separated from the coal and its own dross, being very heavy falls down to a trench made to receive it at the furnace hole below. This liquid metal I saw them shovel up with an iron shovel, and so pour it into moulds, in which it cools, and so they take it thence in sort of wedges, or pigs I think they call them. It is a fine metal in its first melting, looks like silver.

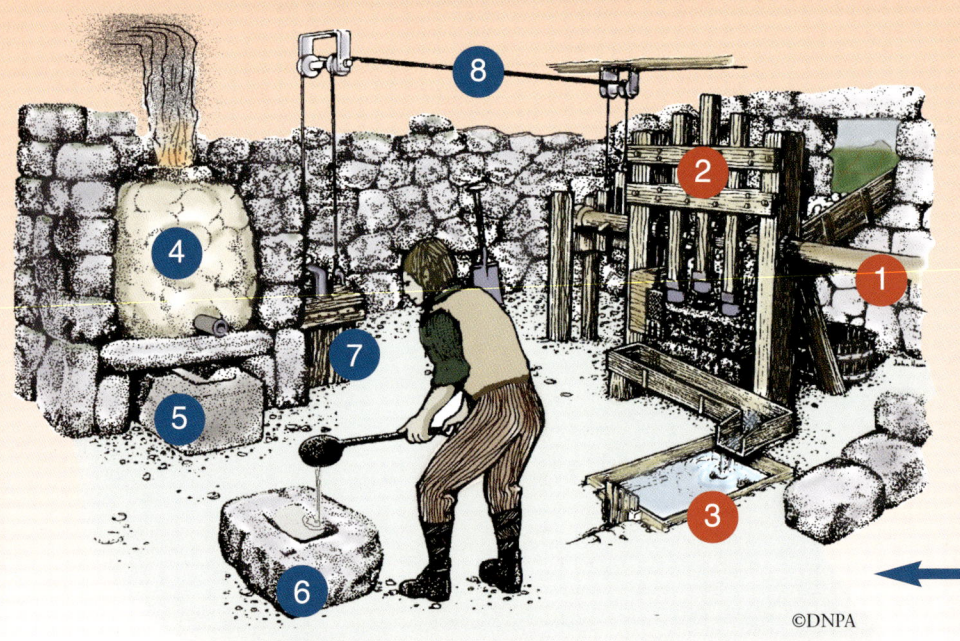

COMPOSITE INTERPRETATION OF TIN DRESSING AND SMELTING ACTIVITES

Robert Burnard's photograph of the remains of the blowing house above Merrivale Bridge, looking west, taken in May 1889. Right is his 1887 photograph of the remains of the wheel pit at Weeke Ford, Chagford and, below, his 1887 photo of the furnace and chimney in the ruins of the blowing house at Hartor.

Writing in July 1891, the antiquarian and photographer Robert Burnard describes the remains of a blowing house:

At one end of the ruin huge stones are built up, forming what was once a furnace, with flues leading to the exterior of the hut. A little farther up the slope is another ruin, which was evidently a dwelling with a small wheel-pit by its side, wherein revolved the wheel which worked the bellows used for exciting the heat in the furnace below. Here lived and worked the 'white' tinners, who received from the 'black' tinners the ore which the latter had won from the tin-bearing alluvial ground.

Though often found in close proximity, surviving tinners' buildings on Dartmoor are of two main distinct types: blowing houses and stamping mills. Opposite is an artist's composite interpretation of activities illustrating what when on in each; the red numbers pertaining to the stamping mill, blue to the blowing house. Water wheels provided power and remains of their wheel pits can still be seen.

KEY: 1. The wheel shaft bringing power to operate the stamps. 2. Here three head of stamps are used to crush the ore into fine particles prior to smelting. In some instances stamps would stand alone and not in a mill building. 3. Collecting pit for capturing the crushed ore from the stamps. 4. The furnace which contains tin ore and fuel, with air blown in by bellows. 5. The hearthstone and trough in which the molton tin is received. 6. A mould stone into which the tinner is pouring molten tin to make an ingot. 7. The bellows, here driven by an arrangement of pulleys attached to the water wheel shaft. 8. A pulley system rigged in the roof of the blowing house to drive the bellows (various methods were employed).

That Ashburton had become a flourishing market town by the early twelfth century is evident from a deed which was discovered in the Buckfast Abbey Cartulary by which Roger de Nunant 'for the safety of his soul and that of his wife Alice' granted to the monks his lands of Sideham, while reserving for himself and his men the right of using a ford across the Dart 'for going to market at Ashburton'. This deed cannot be later than King John which proves that the town was a trading centre soon after the Conquest and had been in Saxon times, this giving the Portreeve his title.

Certain it is that soon after the Bishop of Exeter took possession of the Manor, Ashburton became a Stannary and a centre of the wool trade.

The Stannary is mentioned in one of the very earliest of our mining records, a letter in the Black Book of the Exchequer concerning proceedings of William de Wrotham, appointed Custos, or Keeper, of the Stannaries in place of Geoffrey Fitz Peter, Justiciary of England in 1197.

William de Wrotham wasted no time. On 19 January 1198, he took the Stannaries of Devon in hand, and with the Sheriff and various men of note 'made enquiry on oaths of twenty-six wise discreet jurors concerning weights by which tin was accustomed to be weighed and custom to the king paid'. The jurors were Ashburton's Osbert and John Prigge (relations no doubt), Walter le Bon of Totnes, and Alured of Brent. In this document elaborate regulations were laid down for the Stannaries, including the system of coinage in force until 1838.

The twelfth century brought great prosperity to Ashburton, for not only tin but the wool trade, fostered by the monks of nearby Buckfast Abbey which had been refounded in 1137, was flourishing and expanding. Within easy reach of Exeter and the port of Dartmouth, this little Westcountry town, in the years when Roger de Nunant and his men travelled here to the market, must have been a bustling place especially at the time of the coinage and the wool clip. Foreign tongues would have mixed with the slow burr of the moor, as grand European merchants and grimy tinners jostled round the Bull Ring; pack-horses pushed their way down the narrow streets; traders cried their wares from wayside booths, and scruffy tinners' dogs scavenged through the inevitable garbage of the gutters. It was at this time that Ashburton, because it was the Royal Manor and the most productive and important of the four Devon Stannaries, became a town of international significance.

King John had given the Stannaries a Charter and his son, Richard Earl of Cornwall, determined to put that Charter to good effect. This able man, so different from his lethargic brother, Henry III, resembled much more in intellect and ambition his nephew King Edward I. But, as a younger son, he had to look overseas for his kingdom, and he was, like his grandfather, the first Angevin sovereign, a European.

In 1250, the Emperor Frederick II died, and with him the Hohenstaufen dynasty. There followed 'the terrible interregnum of the Empire' which lasted until the installation of Rudolf of Hapsburg in 1275. During this period the

Electors became the most sought after men in Europe, and there was a rush of candidates from near and far, pitting their claims against each other, and pledging enormous sums in an effort to buy the Crown of Charlemagne. Among these candidates was Richard of Cornwall, great grandson of the Empress Matilda, determined to become the first English Emperor and ready to purchase his empire with the revenues of his earldom. Tin now became the 'Imperial metal', heavy burdens were laid upon the tinners of the Royal Manor, and the lodes were worked until they could yield no more. At immense expense Richard obtained the title 'King of the Romans', and in 1257 with unparalleled splendour, he was crowned at Aachen. But though now heir apparent, he never got his empire. He visited Germany on a number of occasions but the Germans, having his money, lost interest in him, and the sacrifice had been made to no purpose.

How much his deprivations contributed to the gradual decline of the Stannary it is hard to say. Activity continued on a reduced scale for many years to come, and the Coinage Roll of 1303, the earliest statistical record of our mines in existence, gives details of the Ashburton coinage (see Appendix 2). In that year the total quantity of tin raised in Devon was 40½ tons, of which Ashburton contributed 21½ tons as compared with Chagford 17½ and Tavistock 1½.

The Stannary continued to hold foremost place, and in 1327 one 'William de Somerhill of Ashburton, held an important office under the Crown in connection with the Devon mines. In 1391 an Act of Parliament decreed that tin could only be shipped out of the realm from Dartmouth, which was Ashburton's nearest port, but this act was not a success as it only lasted a year, and was then rescinded. Exeter Cathedral too evidently found the proximity of this Stannary convenient, as the accounts of 1372–3 show that tin for two bells was bought from William Ryka of Ashburton at 2d per ton, and copper from John Brasyer of Dartmouth at 3½d.

All this time the wool trade was on the up and up. Edward I had relieved wool of taxes and granted Charters to foreign merchants, encouraging them to settle in England and obtain skilled cloth artisans. Ashburton, handy to the port of Dartmouth, was not only well placed for the boom, it now had a friend in high places.

Dartmouth harbour mouth and castle.

Opposite: The seal of Richard of Cornwall.

Bishop Stapledon.

Walter Stapledon was born during the latter half of the thirteenth century probably at his father's house of Stapledon near Holsworthy. Having the advantages of good birth, and an excellent education, he became, in quick succession, Professor of Canon Law at Oxford, Precentor of Exeter, Rector of Aveton Gifford, and some time before 1307, Chaplain to Pope Clement V. In 1308, he was elevated to the See of Exeter as the fifteenth Bishop. His reign of eighteen and a half years was outstanding in the history of the diocese; and his achievements are evident to this day, for he was responsible for the rebuilding of the cathedral and the erection of the Bishop's Throne, the enclosure at its base being approached by three steps of black marble from the Ashburton quarries.

Bishop Stapledon loved Ashburton, and the Ashburton people loved him. The site of his residence, was bound to the east by Woodland Road, and to the west by St Lawrence Street, later occupied by the Fleece Inn. An entrance to the palace enclosure is said to have been beneath an archway once situated in East Street twenty yards from the turning to St Lawrence Lane.

The good Bishop spent what were probably his happiest days as benefactor to the town, which was so dear to him. Here, in 1310, he made provision for fairs and markets, and in 1313, admitted James de Champenie as vicar. The following year, he founded the Guild of St Lawrence and bestowed 'the Chapel, just completed within the boundary of his court, upon condition that the said Guild should find a priest, who should pray for his soul and those of his predecessors and successors, for donors of land, and other benefactors, and keep a free school'. The stipend was to be £14.13s. per annum. The fraternity land was valued at £10.15s., and the balance was to be spent in 'repacion and maintainance of ledes for the construction of pure and wholesome water to the town of Aysheperton and upon relief and sustenacion of such persons as are affected when plague is in the town that they, being from all company, may not affect the whole.'

On the Eve of the Assumption in 1314, the Portreeve and Commonality of Ashburton, under their common seal, testified their acceptance of the Bishop's offer. This Charter is preserved in the Devon Heritage Centre at Exeter.

The chantry was suppressed under Henry VIII, but the school carried on, and in 1593, when the Chapel and land were bought back, the Portreeve and Burgesses established a Grammar School which continued until 1928.

Only the fourteenth century tower of the chapel now remains. It is still one of the principal features of Ashburton and figures in the Arms of the Borough, which depicts St Andrews Church with his cross and a teasel plant along with the sun and moon: motto: *Fides probate Coronat*. The teasel, sun and moon are said to represent Ashburton's sources of prosperity, wool, copper and tin.

On 3 April 1314, Bishop Stapledon declared that the parish church had become very dilapidated and must be restored. The north aisle was rebuilt in 1315, and, following complaints of a deficiency by the Bishop, sacred ornaments were ordered to be supplied and a new vestry built. (This vestry has now disappeared and there is some doubt as to its actual site.)

In medieval times, the church boasted five altars, and the high altar was separated from the nave by a handsome screen surmounted by a rood. Though these furnishings were destroyed in the sixteenth century, much remains in this fine church to bear witness to the zeal of Bishop Stapledon and the prosperity of the borough during the Middle Ages.

Chapel of St Lawrence tower.

The Bishop had now risen to the highest office in the land, Lord Treasurer of England under Edward II, and one of the few loyal and high principled men supporting this unsatisfactory King. In September, 1324, he was compelled to leave Exeter for official duties and was away for two years. In September, 1325, with Edward Prince of Wales, he did homage for Aquitaine and Poitou to the King of France, and, while he was there, Queen Isabella tried to inveigle him into the plot against her husband. That he refused, and escaping to England warned the King, is obvious from a letter Edward II wrote to his French brother-in-law, Charles le Bel, on 1st December, 1325, 'The Honourable Father in God, Walter, has returned, having certified to us that his life was in peril from some of our banished enemies.'

From this time the Bishop viewed the future with foreboding, and an atmosphere of sadness and farewell overshadowed his last visit to Exeter on September 22nd, 1326. Sure enough Queen Isabella, with her lover Mortimer and a rebel force, landed in Sussex six days later.

King Edward promptly committed London to the custody of Bishop Stapledon, who solemnly excommunicated the rebels, before returning to the capital. Unfortunately, this was no deterrent to the Queen's advance, nor to the Londoners who rose in her support. As the Lord Treasurer rode to dinner at his home at Eldedeneslane (Old Deans's Lane), he and his party were set upon by the mob and lynched. His head was carried to the Queen at Gloucester, his dishonoured body, and those of his two squires, buried in a rubbish dump. Not until later was he given a Christian burial when his remains were translated to Exeter Cathedral and interred on the north side of the chancel, where his effigy and memorial remain.

Nowhere was the news of this horrible murder received with deeper grief than at Ashburton, where the Bishop is today commemorated in the north aisle of the church, in St Lawrence's Tower, and in the Arms of the Borough.

But now the rebellion was over, and a new reign had begun, which was to bring unprecedented wealth to the wool staplers and cloth merchants of England. No fewer than nine statutes of Edward III deal with the wool and cloth trade, and the boom continued through the fifteenth century, regardless of the turmoil of the Wars of the Roses, as is evident from the quantities of statutes enacted, some of these coupling tin with wool. Between 1378 and 1485 thirty Acts came on to the statute book relating to the marketing and export of wool, cloth and tin, the rights and facilities of foreign merchants to buy in British markets but not to import foreign cloth, contracts, and the quality of goods shipping through English ports to Calais, now also English and the seat of the Staple.

The Hundred Years War brought a certain stagnation of trade, but Ashburton determined to carry on, as is evident from a petition to Richard II 'praying that as a Royal Manor the inhabitants be granted rights of freedom from toll in all

markets.' His successor took note of this petition for among the records of the Court of Chancery is Patent Roll No 3 of Henry IV.

'We command that you permit the Manor of Ashburton which is of ancient demesne of the Crown of England as by Certification by the Treasurer and Chamberlains of the Lord Richard late King of England and second after the Conquest sent unto his Chancery by order of the same late King fully apparent to quit the like payment of toll to be paid to you according to the custom above said.' Royal patronage certainly had its advantages.

The prosperity of Ashburton continued. The Fulling Mill at Gages (pronounced Gags) a suburb, and Tucking Mill, north of the town, had their origins in these days. But the finest memory of the wool boom is St Andrews Parish Church. Built of granite and dating mainly from the fifteenth century, the wool merchants of Ashburton carried the work begun by Bishop Stapledon to a magnificent conclusion. A notable landmark, clearly visible from the A38 which bypasses the town, is the 90ft high tower, its square shape broken on the north side to provide for the enclosure of the spiral stairway. There is a peal of eight bells, the tenor weighing 22 hundredweight. No doubt some of the tin for these bells was mined locally.

This book is largely a survey of the Medieval Stannaries and with the advent of the sixteenth century, the Middle Ages came to an end. The flourishing cloth industry continued through the Tudor and Stuarts down to the nineteenth century. But though the first recorded Tinners' Parliament sat on Crockern Tor in 1494, the greatest days of the Stannary were ended.

Opposite: This early nineteenth century print of 'The Market Place, Ashburton', conveys something of the bustle around the centre of these small communities. This lively scene complete with pack-horses and traders, would be magnified many times when the miners descended from the moor to have their tin assayed and stamped. The building was demolished in 1848 but in his book Ashburton: The Dartmoor Town, *Francis Pilkington records: 'It is thought the building dated from the fourteenth century. Indeed we may speculate it was built around 1310 when Bishop Stapledon obtained the charter for the Fair.' As described in Chapter 1, in the Stannary towns this 'coinage' traditionally took place at Michaelmas, although it could be held between two and four times a year. The system continued until 1838 when coinage was abolished. Above: Ashburton's current rendering of the ancient Borough Arms.*

Mortar Stones

The instantly recognisable cup-shaped hollows in granite blocks are often found alongside tinner's buildings where the tin-stone was pounded by water-powered stamps. Though not so grand as those illustrated in Bauer's *De re metallica*, published in 1556, the principle in working the stamps was much the same: weighted rods crushing the ore-bearing rock so that the metal element could be separated. Mortar stones were the platform on which the stamp heads fell, creating the typical hollows such as those seen here.

The mortar stones were sometimes turned over to provide a new flat surface and many were discarded when the cavity grew too deep or the stone itself fractured.

opposite page lower: T.A. Falcon's [19]02 photograph of the blowing house [on] the River Meavy under Black Tor. [Th]e two mortars measured 2ft 3in x [1ft] 4in and 2ft 1x1ft 5in and both had [be]en turned and reused with hollows [on] both sides.

[ri]ght: Robert Burnard's photo of a [mo]rtar stone at Hartor blowing house, [ta]ken in December 1887.

[Ab]andoned mortar stones, crazing mill [sto]nes and mould stones are indicators [of] the industry to which many of the [rui]ned buildings on Dartmoor were [on]ce part. Elsewhere these telltale arte[fac]ts are to be found re-used in field [wa]lls and even in farm buildings.

Chapter 5
Ashburton Tin

One of the best known tracks over the moor is the Abbots Way, which winds through some of the most heavily worked of the tin streaming areas. Many a tinner on his path to work would leave home at Ashburton or nearby and follow in the wake of the monks up to the streams, and back again in the evening. In those days it was a busy road; churchmen used it, and pack-horses, labourers, tinners, and moormen of every sort. Today it provides a good hike through lovely scenery.

It enters the moor at Furze Cross, about three miles from Buckfast, winding over Lambs Down, and on to Dean Moor. From the head of the down there is a splendid view across to the reservoir which has drowned not only the old blowing houses of the tinners, but the dwellings of Bronze Age farmers who, long ago, lived and worked in that peaceful valley. The scrub and bracken of Dean Moor cover the remains of past habitation and industry. Its sides are littered with Bronze Age circles and tin streaming works, while up at Huntingdon Cross, by the ford of Avon are nineteenth century warrens and quarry workings. The little river tumbles between wild and lovely banks, as towards its head, the signs of ancient habitation give way to complete emptiness. There are no hut circles here, but burial cairns rise high above the river on Huntingdon Warren, Green Hill and Ryders Hill. Even the rocks have gone, and the streamlet drifts sluggishly through

Aune Head mires and (inset) a tinners' building below Aune Head

damp, flat bogland to Aune (Avon) Head. There is nothing here but moss and rushes, and, overhead, high and shrill, the song of a lark.

Yet long ago, in this remote and desolate place, tinners lived and worked, and the remains of their huts and blowing houses can still be seen with the inevitable piles of spoil, near Fish Lake, a tiny tributary of the Avon. A short distance north of Aune Head is the Sandy Way, which was probably the route by which they brought their tin down to Ashburton.

Continuing its journey between the two Abbeys, the Abbots Way crosses a part of the moor which is not nearly so boggy, for it passes over the Avon at Huntingdon Cross, and winds in the direction of the Erme's tributary, Red Lake, red indeed with peat among the debris left by the streaming. Here in the nineteenth century a new industry, clay mining, took over from tinning. For miles the waste of deserted clay pits litter the area, whilst under Green Hill, a waste tip rises dramatically from the flats below.

The river Erme, one of the most beautiful of all the moorland streams, flows strongly through a quiet and peaceful plain. From Harford the river bubbles and gurgles between Harford Moor and Stall Moor until the steep hill sides give way to the broad basin of Erme Plains, to meander through clumps of rush and sedge, soundless save for the munch of cows and the whirr of dragonfly wings. Perhaps it was the same peace and beauty that attracted the Bronze Age settlers three thousand years ago, for remains of their huts, cairns and burials cists can be seen right up the banks to Erme Head. Cattle have grazed on these pastures from early times to the present, and needless to say, the tinners are everywhere in evidence. The valley was anything but peaceful then. There are little piles of blue grey gravel, thrown up in every tributary and gully round old blowing houses, covered now with bracken and moss. Just beyond Red Lake is another little tributary called

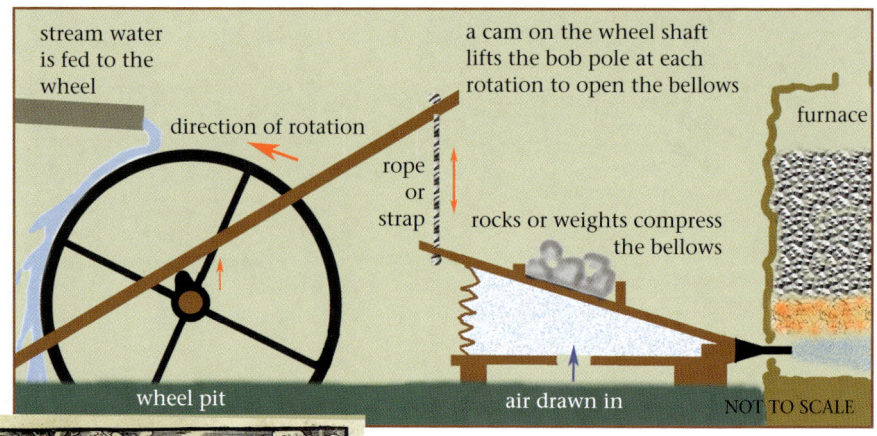

As with the arrangement of the stamps within the blowing house, the mechanism for working the bellows varied. The 1556 drawing (left) from De re metallica *shows the bellows being worked by hand, but on Dartmoor where streams were plentiful, a waterwheel usually drove both stamps and bellows, the latter forcing air into the cavity below the furnace helping to create the temperatures required to smelt the tin ore. This diagram suggests one way in which this could be achieved; elsewhere systems of ropes, pulleys and rods might be employed.*

Hook Lake. Here is an example, which is interesting, of a blowing house, which can be dated by documentary evidence to at least 1661, for in a lease of that date, it is described as 'a certain Tynwork called or house by the name of Hook Lake situate within the parishes of Brent and Ugborough and within the jurisdiction of the Stannary Courts of Plympton and Ashburton.'

Above Erme Head, and following Blacklane Brook to its sources, the traveller nears one of the most dangerous areas of Dartmoor.

Robert Burnard's 1889 photo of the blowing house 'close to the junction of Hook Lake with the Erme'. A mould stone (circled) lies among the ruins.

Burnard's 1905 photograph shows the mine-workings at Gobbett Mine looking towards Bellever Tor. The mine buildings in the foreground have been demolished. On the right are the remains of the blowing house at Gobbett also pictured in 1905. Circled is the crazing mill used at the site to grind the tin ore before smelting.

Below the industrial complex of former days with its old streamworks, clanging forges and smoking blowing houses, lay the marshland wilderness of Cater's Beam and, beyond, the notorious Foxtor Mires (later to become the prototype of the Great Grimpen mire in *The Hound of the Baskervilles*).

Crazing mill top-stone at Gobbett Mine. In the absence of water power the tin ore would be ground into fine particles between two circular stones, much as the way a miller ground flour. It was a laborious method and largely superceded by stamps.

If one of the old tinners wished to go north to the comparative comfort of Nuns Cross Farm, or make for the tracks of Hexworthy, he could have followed Black Lane, the path of the peat cutters, whose work, like that of the tinners, led them out into the wilds of the moor to stack up their turves. There is a path over Foxtor Mires, but to find it you need to have your wits about you, for to miss your step can lead to trouble.

The river Swincombe rises nearby, and from here a leat was channelled over the downs to Hexworthy, where the tin works were reopened early in the last century. Tin had been exploited here hundreds of years earlier, and just where the track meets the road, lie the remains of two interesting blowing houses known locally as Gobbett Mine and Deep Swincombe. The Gobbett stones were first accurately surveyed and recorded in 1870 by Avery who was told by a

65

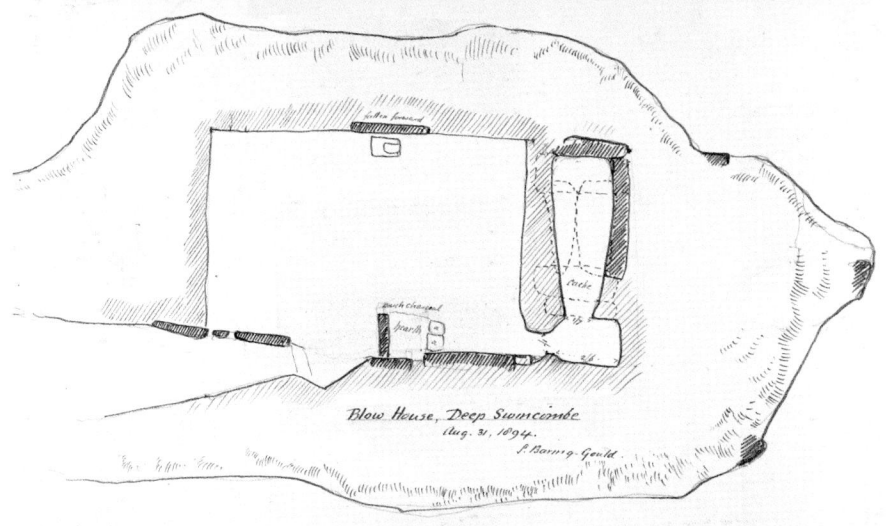

miner that 'there were some stones in large piles of rubbish at Gobbets Mine'. The actual blowing house had disappeared, its stones having been removed for building, but the mill, mortar and mould stones remained, and they are there today, their age being about four hundred years.

Not far from Gobbett is Deep Swincombe blowing house. Its former function has been questioned. Was it used for smelting or housing pigs? Swincombe means 'Valley of Swine'. Some experts believe the large stone outside the house to have been a pig trough, while others suggest it was the trough that collected molten tin beneath the furnace, and that these ruins really are those of a blowing house. The little stream trickling down the edge of Deep Swincombe is called the O Brook (Wobrook). At the top of the hill are the remains of Henroost and Hooten where tin was mined extensively. The nineteenth century shafts were sunk in old works that had been there since the Middle Ages.

The miners at Henroost had a choice of blowing houses to which they could take their tin, for they were within easy reach of either Swincombe or Week Ford on the banks of the Dart. Here in a sheltered valley, among trees and bracken are the two ruins, almost touching, but not necessarily in use at the same time. These are known as Beara House and Mill. The first a

Top: Revd S Baring-Gould's plan of the 'Blow House' at Deep Swincombe, dated 1894. The hearth is shown and at the right what is described as a 'cache'.

Right: This is said to be the tinners' trough at Deep Swincombe, lying near the blowing house. It is too large for a mould stone and perhaps is the trough set at the foot of the furnace to collect the molten tin.

blowing house and the second a stamping mill. Nature is taking over now, and both are fast disappearing, for earth and moss half cover the mortar stones, and trees and shrubs push through walls, windows, and lintels. A large oak tree growing through one of the ruins, gives a clue as to when these buildings were last used. On the hillside, just above, is a hut circle to which a gable end was added at a later date. Here it was, according to tradition, that the old men stored their tools, using it as a cache.

Round the bend of the river is a centuries-old meeting place for all and sundry, now a tourist hot-spot, Dartmeet. By the side of the main bridge lies the ancient clapper, which probably dates from the thirteenth century, where the pack-horses used to cross in the days when they carried wool and other goods from Tavistock to Bovey Tracey, for this was one of the principal routes over the moor. Veering off to Chagford just east of Merrivale, it went south to North Hessary Tor, and via Swincombe to Dartmeet clapper. Thence it can be traced along modern roads and lanes, over Ponsworthy Bridge to Widecombe, past the heights of Rippon Tor and Haytor, down to Bovey and away to Exeter. Pack-horses were used for the main routes, but it is possible they employed other means of carrying tin from the more remote moor. In 1829 Moore in his *History of Dartmoor* relates that 'at present the use of the pack-horse still avails and the produce of the fields are all conveyed on horseback, sledges or sledge carts are also used, drawn chiefly by oxen, sledges are seen at work on many steep fields.' Mrs Bray mentions a woodcut she was shown of dogs pulling a sledge with little bags of tin upon it. Thus it might have been that some tinners carried their ore along the Sandy Way, over to Foxtor Mires, for smelting and stamping.

An artist's view of the old clapper bridge and the later arched bridge at Dartmeet. These ancient clappers, constructed from locally available granite, served as river and stream crossing into antiquity, to be largely replaced by modern arched bridges in the nineteenth century.

On this part of the moor, the greatest tin centre is Widecombe, its debt to the ore that made it rich proclaimed by the magnificent tower, one of the finest in the Westcountry, which soars up from its handsome church. Inside, the so-called tinners' rabbits run their eternal circle round one of the roof bosses.

There is a track to Widecombe from the Ancient Tenements. It runs from the Wallabrook round the south of Hamel Down to Widecombe village and was known, certainly in 1491, as the Church Way. From this route there are magnificent views over the moor, and, towards the Warren House Inn, some spectacular tin workings are to be seen, for here mining has changed the face of the moor.

At the foot of Golden Dagger and Birch Tor lie the earliest medieval streamworks, as the gullies, shafts and deep gurts of the later mines change the whole silhouette of the hill towards Challacombe and up to Grimspound. Here, through the valley below the Warren House Inn, the Wallabrook brought power for smelting, evident in the remains of blowing houses on its banks. One of them was near Runnage Farm, where a large mortar stone, now part of a drystone wall, stares incongruously at the passer by.

The Warren House Inn originally got its name from a rabbit warren, and so back we come to the old connection between rabbits and tin. They are carved on the roof bosses at Widecombe and Chagford, other parish churches in Devon, and elsewhere. In the early Middle Ages these three rabbits, joined in a triangle by their ears, were a symbol of the cult of Venus, so when they began to appear in churches, a new meaning had to be found for them and the Holy Trinity seemed the

The view across Headland Warren Farm towards Hookney Tor and Grimspound. The valley sides here are riven with deep gullies or 'gurts', the work of early miners following the lodes of ore from the valley floor. Nearby are the remains of the rabbit warrens, specially constructed mounds in which the animals were 'farmed'. Inset: Warreners marked their boundaries in much the same way as tinners – this 'Warren Bounds' stone is one of thirteen at Headland, dating from c.1780.

The 'Tinner's Rabbits' roof boss (left) in Widecombe church. The link between tin miners and this symbol is a tenuous one and, indeed, the animals represented are quite possibly hares, not rabbits. But the legends persist and the symbol occurs widely on the moor, not only in art (such as the painting 'Magical Moon Hares' by Dartmoor artist Eleanor Ludgate) but more prosaically in inn signs.

obvious answer. Nevertheless, they are far more reminiscent of an ancient fertility symbol, for, from the Palaeolithic Age to the Bronze Age a triangle standing on its apex represented the productive powers of the Mother Goddess. The three rabbits are associated elsewhere with copper, one of the components of bronze, so the producers of the other element, tin, may have co-opted the symbol. Rabbits are also portrayed in religious buildings on the Continent, in the Cathedral at Paderborn in Germany, and at Muota in Switzerland. Perhaps German merchants trading in tin and wool, brought them to England (or took them back again). Coincidentally, Jupiter, whose thunderbolts are the alchemic symbol for tin, has a somewhat unexpected connection with the hare through fable.

But a more pragmatic reason for the Dartmoor tinner's affection for the rabbit was very practical one. He was dependent on them for food, and they provided him with a useful supplementary income. Working as he did, miles from anywhere, the tinner's best means of feeding himself was to breed and trap rabbits. He could make their skins into clothing, and sell any that were left over at the nearest moorland market. The rabbit business was still flourishing in the eighteenth, nineteenth and early twentieth centuries.

Rabbits, we're told, were introduced into this country by the Normans and were certainly bred on the moor in the thirteenth century. Trowlesworthy Warren can be documented to 1292, and some time before that date, Samson de Tracey, who had become lessee of land on the Plym, was granted land at Trowlesworthy for a rabbit warren.

The warrens made by the eighteenth century tinners gave the Warren House Inn its present name. Before that time it was called the New Inn, though there had probably been warrens in the neighbourhood for centuries. The Inn's fame lies chiefly in its peat fire which is said never to have been extinguished. It has a fine southward prospect, and around the slopes on which it stands are the Vitifer,

Rabbit Warrens

There is a link between rabbits and tinners more prosaic than theories based on fertility symbols and church roof bosses. The high moor, where streamed tin was abundant, provided clear ground and unlimited granite from which to build the foundation for warrens, or 'buries', used for farming rabbits on a large scale. The open moor was also relatively free of predators – and those that did prey on rabbits were at least more visible and easier to catch than in the more wooded lowland valleys. In medieval times both Plympton Priory and Tavistock Abbey held rights from the king to maintain warrens, the animals being a vital food source and valuable for their fur.

Trowlesworthy Warren is said to be the first built, dating from around the end of the thirteenth century, and while the warrens increased in number throughout the medieval period (and survived well into the twentieth century) their basic design remained the same. A core of stone was arranged lengthwise down a slope over which soil and turf was thrown leaving underground burrows accessible to the rabbits. Several such warrens might occupy a single site and these appear in the landscape today as 'pillow mounds'.

Above: A medieval manuscript depicting rabbits being trapped in a warren using a ferret to drive the animals into a net. Below: The warren house at Ditsworthy is one of only two surviving on Dartmoor (the other being Trowlesworthy) and here, in the distant hillside the distinct outline of a warren can be seen. Inset: A vermin trap on Legis Tor. Several types of trap were used by warreners to catch predators such as stoats and weasels.

Hut at Wistmans Warren c.1900 is one of the few to be photographed and no trace of it now remains. Elsewhere on the moor rough stone shelters are associated with the work of the warrener and it's possible such accommodation was shared with tin streamers.

On lowland farms, the rabbit was considered part of the annual 'crop' and they were nurtured and regularly harvested, several hundred being caught on even small farms each year, often using tame ferrets or polecats, snares and gin traps. In the early years of the twentieth century at Southcombe Farm, Widecombe, over 900 rabbits were caught annually and taken to market. At this time the coming of the railway had greatly increased the demand for rabbit meat in cities and thus piqued the farmers' interest in maintaining rabbit populations. It seems inevitable that much of the miner's meat diet would comprise rabbit in one form or another.

Ancient Bennett's Cross (inset) was used as a convenient boundary marker for the Headland warreners who inscribed this and other stones with the letters 'WB' to delineate the extent of their boundaries. Rabbits remained much-prized by butchers well into the last century and here baskets of rabbits are being put aboard a London-bound train at North Tawton station in the 1920s.

The Warren House Inn (centre left) standing amid mine workings and miners' barrack buildings. The first inn on the site is thought to date from around 1760 but at the time this photograph was taken, c.1910, its best custom came from the men working in the Vitifer, Birch Tor and Golden Dagger mines. Below: Burnard's photograph of Chaw Gully taken in 1894. The figure standing at the foot of the gully is the Revd Sabine Baring-Gould whose novel Guavas the Tinner, published a year before this photo was taken, contains a pivotal scene based on this early mine working.

Birch Tor, and Golden Dagger mines where they worked tin from medieval to modern times. Chaw Gully cuts deep into the middle of this ancient complex, its origins reputedly going centuries back in time. Above it runs a Bronze Age triple stone row, later cut in half by the tinners.

This is the land whose tin made Widecombe rich, and raised the 'Cathedral of the Moor'. Extensive studies in the area around the village have revealed a number of medieval sites and ruined dwellings. Some can be dated from documentary evidence, a few of these references giving the exact dates and positions of tin works and blowing houses. It is fascinating and exciting to trace the paths of the 'Old Men of the Moor' from these ancient references. One of the most interesting concerns Blackaton blowing house, which is mentioned in a survey of 1500, 'Lord Dinham's Landes'. The site is clearly indicated and

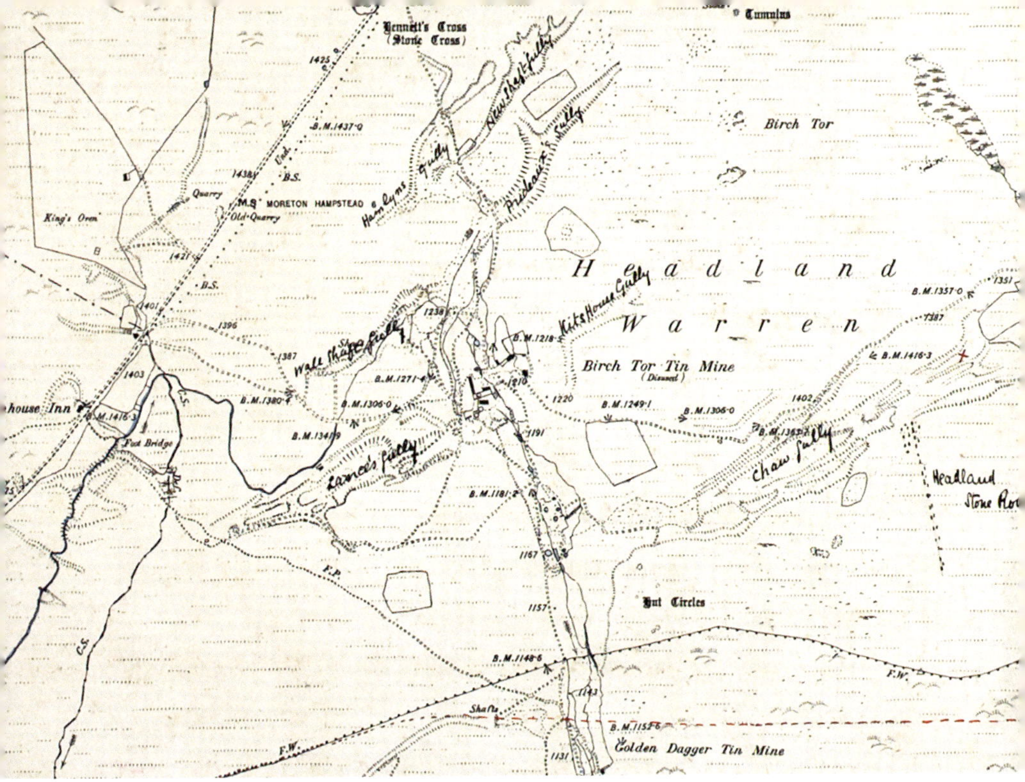

Above: Robert Burnard's OS maps, now in the Dartmoor Archive, were often annotated with details of artefacts in the landscape. In this portion of an 1885 map showing Birch Tor and Golden Dagger mines he notes the names given to the principle open workings: Hamlyn's Gully, Prideaux's Gully, Lance's Gully and Chaw Gully etc. *Below:* A remarkable photograph from the Taylor Collection reveals the devastation to the moorland landscape wrought by opencast mining. This is at Vitifer Mine taken c.1920s.

the stamping mill was evidently in use before 1566. Here still is the deep pear-shaped hollow which once contained the mill pond, and the leat which fed the pond can also be traced from a small stream above. The tin smelted here was probably brought from the open gullies, still to be seen on the Stoneslade hillside.

There is another blowing house on Blackaton Ball Moor, on the left hand side of the river Webbern. Excavations have revealed it, and also its separate channels communicating with the river, as well as a leat, which runs round the side of 'the Ball' and ends on the south side of the hill. The northernmost channel was for the tailway of the leat, the southernmost for the feed to the waterwheel.

From Widecombe and over Hamel Down towards Kings Tor the remains of many small workings can be found, these being the activities of seasonal tinners. When the lodes had been worked right up to the hilltops, and high above the sources of stream water, pear-shaped ponds were dug to collect the rain, and the channels leading to them are still there, round the crest of the hill and clearly visible from Hamel Down.

Even the tin workings of one man could involve quite complicated hydraulics. On the south side of Kings Tor, for instance, there is a digging only twenty to thirty yards long, and, into this leads a channel, issuing from a small spring known as Haswell. It is only wet in winter, in spring, or in a very rainy summer, and this goes to show the toughness of the tinner, for work in this particular place was impossible unless the weather was really nasty! The dry season was smelting and stamping time.

While mining, along with wool, brought prosperity to Dartmoor, helping to finance the building of churches such as St Pancras in Widecombe, the miners themselves seldom got rich.

Chapter 6
Chagford: The Market of the Moor

Above: One of the earliest known photographs of Chagford showing the upper square c.1860. This is the somewhat dilapidated scene that would have been familiar to miners coming to town to purchase goods and food. Below: The Three Crowns inn is more representative of Chagford today, well placed to serve a buoyant tourist industry.

While much has changed in Chagford in recent years through the introduction of new housing, the market town retains a good deal of its former charm, not least in the historic buildings that stand close to the centre, the solid grey granite church and the medieval buildings nearby.

For those who make the climb to the height of Meldon Common there is a splendid panoramic view of the Chagford district. Far below in the valley are the sites of the Ancient Tenements, inhabited before the thirteenth century, Corndon, Batworthy, Thorn, Yeo and Yardworthy. Far off up on the horizon, on the wildest stretches of the moor, are spread the relics of man's past.

High above Chagford Common looms Kestor, once a place of Iron Age villages, and the huts of iron smiths. Further off is the wilderness of Gidleigh Common leading to Taw Marsh and the peaty heights of Whitehorse Hill and Wild Tor, where the Bronze Age farmers lived.

Robert Burnard's photograph of the remains of Teigncombe Manor, Chagford, taken in 1889. It is said to be the former home of Sir John Whyddon during the reign of Elizabeth I when he made a fortune in the tin industry. Below: The first Chagford Bridge dates from 1224, later rebuilt in the sixteenth century.

As with so many Dartmoor villages, a market, wool, and tin were the elements that supplied Chagford with its fascinating history. But unlike the richer moorland towns, it was the efforts of fifteenth century residents and settlers that led to its prosperity, and not the presence of an ecclesiastical body.

In Saxon times Chagford was the residence of Dodo the Saxon, and after the Conquest, it was given by William I to the Bishop of Coutances in Normandy. In the Domesday Survey there are references to various manors in the parish. Chagford, Taincombe (Teigncombe), Rushford, South Teign and Shapley. Old farmhouses still exist on their original sites, solidly fixed upon their ancient foundations. Chagford was fortunate in that it lay on a main pack-horse route from Exeter. This, coupled with its proximity to rich tin lodes, led to its growth as a major market town. As early as the twelfth century the Lord of Chagford, recognising the town's potential, was given royal assent to hold a market, and he followed this up by building Chagford Bridge which has spanned the Teign since

Samuel Prout's 1811 etching of the later bridge dating from c.1600.

St Michael's church, Chagford, benefited considerably from tin mining for not only did the tinners pay an annual tithe but in 1480 records show the church received direct revenue from 'the tinworks at Bubhyll'. In her book A History of Chagford, *Jane Hayter-Hames relates that 'John Westcott, jnr. His will, dated 1522, leaves to the Store of St Michael a half share of a tin works called Shylston Beme'.*

1224, and possibly before. By this time the population was expanding, forty prospectors and those who sought prosperity by sheep farming and wool trading had settled in the so-called Ancient Tenements in the valleys around the town.

Chagford now had enough people and enough money with which to build its new church, which was dedicated to St Michael in 1261. Here visitors can see the tinners' rabbits represented on a roof boss, their somewhat dubious place in the story of tin related earlier.

Chagford was one of the three original Devon Stannary towns, and the statute of Edward I (1305) gave it the right to select, and send, twenty-four stannators or jurymen to the Tinners' Parliament. The Chagford area covered the north-eastern quarter of the moor, and the town saw its period of greatest prosperity during the mid-fourteenth century when, in 1385, it took first place in the production of tin. This prosperity extended into the mid-fifteenth century, and it was during these years that the main part of the present church was erected, the magnificent tower rising as a symbol of the town's importance. In those days Chagford was known as 'the Market of the Moor', for, not only did it have a weekly market, but also four fairs on the feast days of St George, St Michael, St Luke and Our Lady. Even in the 1800s tinners were still coming in to buy household provisions, meat, vegetables, and earthenware, and were selling tin and farm produce.

Tin played an intrinsic part in the life of Chagford and its neighbourhood. The principal occupations of the majority of the parishioners were cattle and sheep

Fun & Games

'The eleventh month November, the nights are cold and long,
We'll go into the ale house and spend our nights in song.
We'll sit about the fire, we'll cider drink and ale,
We'll kiss the pretty maidens, and tell a merry tale.
Folk song collected by Revd Baring-Gould from J. Potter of Postbridge, 1888.

While the tinners were much a law unto themselves, their place in Dartmoor society was cemented by the fact that many were local men with close family connections. While their behaviour might occasionally overstep the mark, generally they were held in high regard. Certainly they were welcome at the inns and alehouses for they were, by repute, hard drinkers – and only later did the Wesleyan influence and the effects of Methodism see the rise of Temperance houses and consequent abeyance in drunkeness.

Alehouses and small 'winks' provided ample opportunities for refreshment and socialising. Towns such as Ashburton had upwards of twenty or so known 'houses' in the sixteenth and seventeenth century. Church Houses brewed their own ale and, as the church also received tithes from tin, so a centuries-old tie persisted between the tinner and the parson.

Beside those in the towns, early hostelries were sited along the packhorse routes, providing sustenance for passing trade. Many are now gone, such as 'Newhouse' whose ruins stand beside the road near Cold East Cross, or they simply became dwellings like the isolated cottage at Hound Tor or the old Greyhound Inn at Postbridge. Here miners could meet friends over a pint (cider or ale) and play cards – euchre being a favourite – or join in songs well known to all.

Burnard's photo of the Greyhound Inn, Postbridge, 1892.

All that remains of the former 'Newhouse' inn on Blackslade Down near Haytor.

Country sports, where time allowed, were the principal outdoor pastime. Many countrymen kept a terrier or two for hunting foxes, badgers and otters, indulging in sports now long since forbidden. With most of the moorland streams inhabited by brown trout, with runs of sea trout and salmon too, a spot of poaching would supplement the pot.

Dan'l Leamon in 1888 whom Burnard described as 'a regular old Moorman, not innocent it is said of a little occasional poaching.'

By the mid nineteenth century wrestling had become rather more sophisticated than the rough and ready bouts enjoyed by the miners and, where kicking shins was allowed, leather gaiters replaced the 'bands of hay'. Right: Abraham Cann is the most celebrated of Devon wrestlers – Champion of All England – who in 1826 fought in front of a crowd of 12 000 near Devonport.

But it was wrestling that was considered the miners' sport. Writing at the end of the 1600s historian Richard Carew describes a wrestling match and considers it to be an 'activity of Devon and Cornish men in this faculty of wrestling beyond those of other shires'. Though the subject of much argument, the styles of wrestling differed little between the two counties, as one writer puts it 'the Devonshire bout was characterised by kicking and tripping, while the Cornishmen were noted for hugging and heaving'. The Revd Baring-Gould, however, describes the more brutal form of wrestling practised in Devon:

> The Devonshire wrestlers wore boots soaked in bullocks blood and indurated at the fire, and with these hacked the shins of their opponents, who wore as a protection 'skillibegs', or bands of hay twisted and wrapped around their legs below the knee.

farming, and also tin washing, and the same was true of the richer landowners, for it is probable that they also, not only owned, but worked the farms on their manors. The early moorland farmers needed to be skilled in leading water for drainage and irrigation, and these same talents must have proved useful in the construction of leats and the diversion of water courses for stream tinning. Not that they were always put to good use. In 1431 Thomas Smythe and Henry Verdaer were fined at Chagford's Manor Court for diverting the course of the town's water supply, and in 1432 the same pair were fined again, for neglecting to pay the Lord of Chagford for use of his furnace or oven. This may refer to a blowing house, as the Lord to whom it belonged would be owed a proportion of the smelted tin.

Even up to 150 years ago there were many small time farmers-cum-tinners, eking out a living by renting rabbit warrens, keeping pigs and hens, and selling heather honey from their bee hives. The pig would be killed before Christmas, and salted down for the winter, and skins of rabbit and sheep made into warm clothing. The women of the family would spin and knit the wool from the fleeces and would plait barley straw into bonnets, skirts, and mats. Out on the open moor the hardy husbandmen waited upon the rains, the water pouring down the hillsides making stream tinning possible. It was a spartan existence, but the moor men of the Middle Ages were a tough breed.

On market and fair days, surplus produce was loaded on to pack-horses with the help of pack-saddles and the accompanying furniture of crooks or crubs. Thus burdened they made their way through the tangle of high-hedged narrow lanes that have led off the moor and down to Chagford since Saxon times. They are still there and so is the little market square, but in medieval times it must have appeared very different, especially on the days when tin was weighed and assayed to be purchased by rich merchants or agents of the king. A strangely incongruous

'Chagford' an etching by Samuel Prout 1811, said to be Teignhead Farm, close to the tin-rich headwaters of the North Teign.

assembly milled about Chagford, smartly dressed strangers with foreign accents rubbing shoulders with rough-spoken hoary moor men, as the cheapjacks cried their wares, and the pack ponies shuffled in the dust.

Not all the Chagford parishioners, of course, were primitive farmers, for there were well established prosperous families in the neighbourhood, as many a fine old barton testifies to this day. Chief among these were the Wibberys, ancestors of the first Lord of Chagford, and the Prouses, who owned the manors of Gidleigh and Throwleigh and resided for many generations at Waye Barton.

In Richard II's reign the Moores were prominent, settling at Rushford Barton. In the thirteenth and fourteenth centuries, anticipating the possibility of tin profits, immigrant 'foreigners' arrived to occupy the so-called Ancient Tenements. Early deeds of these centuries, concerning the property of these families, suggest that some of the richest of the tin deposits were to be found on their lands. A marriage deed of 1224 describes a locality corresponding with the King's Oven area which formed the boundary of Chagford Manor. It concerns one, William Pruz (Prouse), and land called Hurtpyth, which may mean Hurston Moor, the stretch of moorland above Wallabrook which runs to King's Oven, and it suggests that William may have been deriving profits from the tin deposits round Vitifer and Birch Tor (both these works were extensively mined from Tudor to Victorian times). It is known that William had close connections with a certain Fulk Ferrers, a prominent owner of tin works.

In the same year, 1224, Hugh, Lord of Chagford, leased six acres of demesne land to Geoffrey de Pante 'a magna et usferi favea que est mea', (as far as the big old ditch which is mine). Was this a tin working?

The early deeds of the Wibberys, kin to Lord Hugh, bear a crest which appears to be either a cat or a rabbit (a case for more conjecture on the animal's connection with the tin trade?). These old land-owners were doing well in tin, and by the fifteenth and sixteenth centuries such men as John Westcote and William Knapman left wills showing that they had accumulated considerable tin works. The Knapmans were so important in this respect that they became jurats of the Parliament at Crockern, and the Moores of Rushford are listed in 1484 among the Wardens of St Katherine, the Chagford Guild which made large profits from the tin works which it owned.

The Church too, did well out of the industry. Every 'shoveller' (tin worker), had to pay as a tithe to the church, shoveller's penny on all the tin he worked, and various tin works in the area were owned by the parish and church guilds. The parish accounts of the fifteenth and sixteenth century have survived, and they reveal the costs of labour, and the profits and losses of the tin workings. On the whole the profits were not great, but they may have been more substantial in the previous century when Chagford was Dartmoor's leading tin producer.

Ormerod calculated that on average annual profits amounted to £1.2s.6d, the average price of tin being 4d per pound.

The principal tin dealing guild was that of St Katherine, and at Chagford she was revered as the patron saint of tinners. Though the connection between this virgin martyr and tin is not very obvious, she may have been chosen because according to legend, the wheel upon which she was to have been executed was broken by fire from heaven, and as recorded earlier, the alchemic symbol for tin is Jupiter's thunderbolt. On the other hand, St Katherine was frequently invoked against lightning. Tinners working in exposed places may well have sought for protection during the devastating thunderstorms which rocket across the moor. Whatever the reason, she provides a curious connection between the Chagford Stannary, Mount Sinai, and Bonfire Night!

The Chagford Parish Warden Accounts for the years 1480 to 1597 still exist, though with many gaps. There were thirteen Wardens, who under various names, discharged duties similar to those of present day churchwardens. There were also the Way Wardens, Market Wardens, and those of the guilds of St George, St Nicholas, St Eligius, St Anthony and St Katherine, which derived the bulk of their funds from the buying and selling of ale. St Katherine's was the most important of these guilds. It rented the church house, owned a field called St Katherine's Ley, and used its funds for feast day celebrations and payment to the priest for prayers for the souls of its members, and for the address he gave from the pulpit.

Among other items, the accounts of the Wardens and guilds give the names of parts of Chagford parish in which tin was worked, and some of these sites may be the oldest in Devon. The most productive districts lay east of Chagford itself around Great Weeke, Westcott and Drewsteignton, and, from detailed studies of the stream tin lodes, it is evident that tin had been worked in these areas long before 1480. Workings were also located along the Teign Valley from Fingle Bridge up the river to the wild open spaces of Teign Head, amid some of the most spectacular scenery of Devon.

The walker from the height of Prestonbury Castle, ranging across this splendid panorama, can follow the track over the river to the equally prominent

'Near Chagford' an etching by Samuel Prout 1811, reputed to be Manga Farm, now ruined.

William Widgery's 1827 painting of Fingle Bridge and the River Teign.

Cranbrook Castle on the other side, and it will be plain to them that, though no bridge existed at Fingle till 1500, it must always have been a major crossing of the river. Two thousand years ago, the people of the Iron Age sited their two hill-forts to guard this vital ford. The Fishermans Path follows the Teign bank beneath Sharp Tor and Castle Drogo to the site of 'deep works at Parford' and Drogo marsh mentioned in the will of John Westcote in 1522. No visible evidence remains of these works, which are now thickly overgrown with forestry plantation and undergrowth, but careful investigation of the Easterbrook will recall vestiges of the tin works conveyed to William Maule in 1546. This is in the neighbourhood of Rushford Barton, and the buildings now standing on the site are of the usual solid granite and thatch. Tin was streamed elsewhere on the Rushford estates at Coney Ball, recorded as Cony Park (probably a rabbit warren) in the 1539 accounts of St Michael's Wardens.

St Katherine's Guild owned some of the most important tin workings in the immediate vicinity of Chagford. Between the village itself and Westcott, up the slopes of Broom Hill, the fields are seamed with early workings. At Wescott can be seen a deep excavation known as Higher Lines Beam which was probably developed during the late fifteenth and throughout the sixteenth century. Further up the road near Weeke hamlet, tin workings were continued on either side of Weeke Brook. They still remain as huge heaps of rubble and waste, left by the tinners, all those years ago, as they turned up the sand and gravel to get at the ore. Up the valley and into the woods beyond, stretch these pits and open works, dug by 'the old men' as they followed the tin lodes to the surface. West of Great Weeke from Kenslade Lane are deeper open works known as the 'mainlode', but they were excavated in the nineteenth century, and it is these later workings which

Shilstone Farm photographed by R.N. Worth in the 1920s. Close by lies (inset) Bradford Pool the result of early mining activity from which and adit is said once to have passed under the farm itself.

have destroyed the traces of earlier sites. There is however, other evidence. Sometimes the leats that led to the old blowing houses are still visible, though the blowing houses themselves have long since vanished. At Great Weeke Farm, a mortar stone from one of these buildings has been let into an outhouse wall.

But not all the workings were in sheltered surroundings, some of the most prolific lay far out on the wildest parts of the moor. To the north of Chagford, near Shilstone Farm, lies Bradford (or Bradmere) Pool, on the site of the old works, which were conveyed to John Knapman in 1559. During other tin excavations water collected seventy-five feet in depth, they say; and, to this dark and lonely place, made even gloomier by its surrounding trees, came murderers and suicides, giving it a sinister reputation. Once an adit fed from the pool, passing under Shilstone Farm, and acting as a drain, but this has been long blocked up. It was probably the source of the legend that a passage lined with large stones led from Bradmere Pool towards the Teign in the neighbourhood of the logan stone. A similar story tells of another secret passage from Gidleigh Castle to the Teign at Gidleigh Park Bridge, which perhaps also had its origin in mining excavations.

Bleakest and most remote were the tin works on the eastern side of Chagford, where enclosed fields and sheltered bartons give way to open hill slopes rolling into the mists. Here the tinners battled against the cheerless elements, ever mindful of those forefathers who had worked the moor before them. All about them lay traces of prehistoric man. They worked within Bronze Age hut circles, the tors like broken castles looming above them. Near at hand were strange burial cairns and cists, stone rows and circles, relics of an age and peoples unknown.

In the 1522 will of John Westcote, Taw Marsh is mentioned. In medieval times this was a large lake, Steeperton Tor rising high above its head, but over the centuries its bed has filled with sand and gravel. Another mine was sited at Raybarrow Pool, one of the most dangerous bogs on the moor.

It was not only tinners who toiled on these lonely hills. At the height of the moor flourished another now almost forgotten industry. The turf ties above the stream beds were amongst the most productive on Dartmoor, and here, certainly since the reign of King John, and probably before, peat charcoal had been manufactured. Whole tracts of moorland have been completely stripped of their deep peaty covering and left bleak and bare. A landscape of granite and underlying growan, naked to the wind and rain.

The ruins of Knack Mine, one the the moor's most remote mine buildings. First documented in 1799 when operating as Wheal Virgin, it lies among much earlier streamworkings along the infant River Taw. The name is interesting for 'knacking' or 'knocking' mills housed the stamps where the tin ore was crushed, as distinct from blowing houses where it was smelted – although the two operations were sometimes combined. However, Pennington in his book Stannary Law *suggests 'to knack' was to close or abandon a mine.*

Heat & Light

'They burn mostly turves, which is an unpleasant smell, it makes one smell as if smoked like bacon'

Celia Fiennes 1699.

It's likely that the use of peat as a source of heat pre-dates tinning on the moor being so abundant and readily available. However, from the twelfth century onwards in recognition of the value of mining revenue to the King, the formal establishment of laws controlling the activity of miners came into force – this being Stannary Law. This gave miners many privileges not enjoyed by others who worked the land, effectively marking them out as something of a law unto themselves. While the right to forage for fuel predates the Stannaries, there's no doubt that, on the high moor itself, the digging of peat to feed the furnaces of blowing houses, had a significant impact on the landscape. Today of course these extensive peat mires are recognised as being important in the fight against global warming.

While peat, once dried, served well for domestic fires, for smelting purposes it had to be turned into 'coal' through a process of carbonisation. This was achieved much in the same way as wood charcoal is made, through a controlled burning process in granite 'kilns' called meilers, inside which the peat turves were stacked then slowly burned to achieve a hard coke-like material, ideal for use in smelting. Meilers are often found in groups – the one shown is near Wild Tor.

So valuable was peat charcoal that it was transported off the moor in wagonloads, serving the mines of Cornwall and the work of these 'carbonarii' became an important industry of its own, increasing from the twelfth century onwards. Such was the demand that large areas of upland moor still bear evidence of the excavation of peat, in some instances, as in the area between Wild Tor and Quintin's Man, lowering the surface of the moor by several feet.

Steeperton Brook near Wild Tor.

Whatever the time of year, the work of the tin streamers, so closely associated with water, would mean being constantly wet. Those fortunate to work alongside the blowing houses had a least some means of drying their clothes, and it's likely that a number of the ruined dwellings found close to tin streaming works, such as this ruin (left) above the East Dart, were built to provide rudimentary shelter and means of keeping warm.

The eclipse of the Stannaries by the industrial mining companies, whose mine engines ran on coal, did not put an end to the harvesting of peat for domestic use. There were even large-scale, if unsuccessful, operations to industrialise the process. The evidence of this later peat cutting gives some insight into the methods and tools used to cut the peat 'vags' and how they were stacked for drying. Photographs such as those included here help provide some clues in interpreting what remains can be seen on the moor today.

Above: Will May's House, a ruin near Watern Tor, named after a Chagford peatcutter who worked here in the 1780s. Right: Two photos showing the methods of cutting and drying peat.

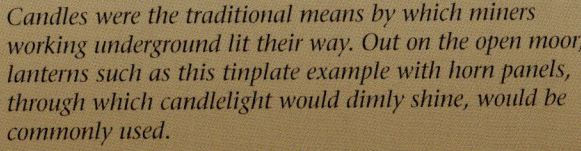

Candles were the traditional means by which miners working underground lit their way. Out on the open moor, lanterns such as this tinplate example with horn panels, through which candlelight would dimly shine, would be commonly used.

Here in those distant days the charcoal burners cut their peat into little bricks, which they dried, piling them into their primitive 'kilns', igniting them from within. Slowly the bricks were carbonized into a blue-grey kind of charcoal. Little is left of them now but for the ruins of meilers constructed from rough moorstone. Only relatively recently has their true use been established and recognised as industrial archeological remains. Rowe and Crossing mistook them for cairns and barrows.

Records imply activity on a huge scale. Henry III in 1219 directed a writ to William de Brimere, Custodian of Lydford Castle, commanding him to permit the men of Eleanor, Queen of England 'to dig, burn and lead away from the turbary of Dartmoor to her Stannary as they used and ought', and in 1222 he directed the bailiffs of Lydford to permit tinners from Cornwall to take carbon from Dartmoor.

This was 'the Black Country' of the Middle Ages. In those days, eight hundred years ago, you could see it all from Cawsand Beacon, Wild Tor, Black Hill, Hangingstone, and Quintins Man; exposed to the four winds of heaven, these kilns glowed and smouldered through the night, while down in the valleys, on the Taw, along Steeperton Brook and around Teignhead, flared the white heat of the blowing house furnaces smelting the 'black tin'. All this is past now, only the barren granite remains where the peat was ripped away, and the odd mould stone lying among the bracken.

To the south of Chagford the land round Fernworthy, the Warren House Inn, and Manaton was, in medieval times, as wild as the eastern moor. There were no reservoirs then, nor forestry plantations. The Warren House Inn had not been built and the B3212 was a muddy track. The granite standing stones were there, along with stone rows and stone crosses, and the tinners took over the Metherall hut circles and used them as stores, and possibly shelters. In one of them a coin of Henry VII was found along with oddments of stream tin, slag and pottery.

The tinners were active along the North Teign to Teignhead. Their delvings scratch the surfaces of Chagford Common, Watern Down and Bush Down, skirting the edges of Grey Wethers and the rows of standing stones of Froggymead and Merripit Hill. The streamworkings of Bush Down and Watern Down Ridge that John Wescote bequeathed in his will of 1522 are visible today. So too are the remains of the blowing houses of medieval Fernworthy. They drowned the hamlet when they made the reservoir, but the site of the blowing house close to the bank, survived. The worthy of Fern was among the lands given by its trustees to John Prouse in 1435. In the seventeenth century it consisted of at least three farms and was known as a village. The lands of Fernworthy were delineated on one side by a tin bound.

Grey Wethers.

Half an hour's walk away is the site of 'Kings Oven', and there has been much speculation as to what exactly this was. It is known only because it is mentioned in the Perambulation of the Forest of Dartmoor made by the king's men in 1240. It was referred to as 'Furnum Regis' in the document and was prominent enough to form a Forest boundary mark. The name suggests that it was some sort of furnace, and its position, in a major tin streaming area, points to it being an ancient smelting house, a place appointed for the second smelting (i.e. before the days of blowing houses) 'at the hiring of the King'. In Crossing's time all that remained was a low rampart of small stones forming a circular enclosure, seventy yards in diameter, in the centre of which was a rounded stone, and near it was a small pile of stones. Baring-Gould in his *Book of Dartmoor*, explains that some of the enclosure's stones had been taken for the erection of mining buildings, and he also mentions a cairn or cist nearby.

Much has been written about the King's Oven, a site linked to the earliest demarcation of Dartmoor's boundaries going back to the Perambulation of 1240. King's Oven was supposed to signify a royal smelting house, constructed in the days when the tin had to be twice smelted, the first time producing ingots containing many impurities which then had to be taken to a place appointed by the King, a Stannary town, to be refined and-coined. The area seen in the photograph lies north of the Warren House Inn. It abounds with gullies of more recent tin workings and the exact site of King's Oven is open to dispute, often confused with the nearby cairn on the summit of Watern Hill.

Visiting the site of Furnum Regis in July 1888, Robert Burnard recorded this 'circular worked stone in the centre of the ruined enclosure. It looks something like the nether stone of a crazing mill,' he notes.

It is not uncommon for prehistoric remains to get a name such as King Arthur's 'Seat or 'Oven', and it may have been to something of this sort that the perambulators referred. We can only speculate, for it is not documented what 'Furnum Regis' actually was.

However, of the four Stannary towns, Chagford is the one which has shown least change. Ashburton, the Royal Manor and busy trading centre, has become a busy little commuter town. The great Abbey at Tavistock and the Priory at Plympton have vanished almost without trace, and Plympton, once a borough in its own right, is now a satellite of Plymouth. But Chagford is still very much part of the moor itself. It boasted no princes or prelates or proud foreign merchants, no warlike de Redvers or high born Courtenays. Its families were of yeoman stock. Prowses, Wibberys and Westcotes, its magnates the tinmen themselves.

Chapter 7
Tavistock and its Great Abbey

It has been described as one of the most delightful towns in Devon, and surely few places can have a more attractive approach. Coming down from the bare uplands of the moor, it appears peaceful among the trees, with hills piling up beyond to the heights above the Tamar valley and the borders of Cornwall.

The river Tavy swishes and ripples under bridges hung with fruit blossom and elder bushes, and past streets and houses built of green volcanic ash-stone from the quarries at Hurdwick, about a mile and a half north of the town.

Except for the fragmentary remains of the former great Abbey and the large medieval parish church, Tavistock is largely a nineteenth century creation, the result of the Victorian copper boom, when Great Consols mine on Blanchdown was one of the richest in Europe. The Duke of Bedford, whose ancestor, Henry VIII's civil servant, got the pickings of the Abbey, was the then 'owner' of the town, and he it was who is largely responsible for most of the buildings we see today. In the 1840s he constructed the canal and workers' cottages, built the large church which has since been taken over by the Roman Catholics, and remodelled the town centre from much of the Abbey site.

The 7th Duke of Bedford's statute, completed in 1864, stands in Bedford Square, Tavistock. Below: The Tavistock canal, opened in 1817, was built to carry copper from the nearby mines to Morwellham Quay, a little over 7km in length.

But, from 1870, recession set in, the mines decayed, and the short-lived copper boom came to an end. It has left behind the haunted Tamar landscape which has a strange and desolate beauty of its own, unique in Devon.

But there was an older and longer-lived prosperity in Tavistock, and even now its memories crop up in unexpected places. In nooks and crannies, are old arches and bits of ancient wall, all that is left of one of the most powerful and famous Abbeys of the Middle Ages.

Its beginnings were in the distant past, in late Celtic times, to be exact, as a small settlement in a hill fort called Trendle. The most westerly of the British tribes, the Dumnonii lived there until the early eighth century, when the Saxons came. It may, in fact, have been one of the last places in Devon to withstand them. The invaders wasted no time in settling there, for it was close to the important central trackway and the river routes of Tavy and Plym. The community which grew up there became known as 'Tavistock', for 'Tavi' was the river valley and 'stoc' refers to an outlying farmstead or hamlet.

The region was at this time poor and scattered, but by the ninth century, there was promise of a better future. Not far away Lydford, thanks to the constructive local government policy of King Athelstan, had been granted the right to a borough court, a market, a mint, and a Portreeve, and traders and settlers were encouraged to come to the town. With this up-and-coming centre so near at hand, traffic increased, for Tavistock lay conveniently on the route from Okehampton into Cornwall.

Meanwhile the Saxons had driven the old native Britons back across the Tamar, and a Saxon thane, Ordgar, had taken up residence at Hurdwick (Ordgarswick). Tradition has it that Ordgar's beautiful daughter was seduced by King Edgar following the murder of her lover, a local farmer. To atone for the crimes of his family Ordgar founded Tavistock Abbey, and endowed it with lands and riches. Thirty-eight years later it was sacked by the Danes.

It survived, however, recovered, and did well. By the twelfth century it was prospering, thanks to a series of Abbots who were also good businessmen, and a

'Tavistock', by Samuel Prout 1811.

potential money-spinner in the shape of the bones of St Rumon. The stream of pilgrims who came to touch these well-promoted relics needed food and lodging for the night, and in their wake arrived traders and victuallers, ready to provide for all, and leave their offerings at the shrine. But the real growth impetus came from the tin industry. Almost on the Abbey steps lay some of the richest lodes in Europe, discovered or rediscovered, during the first years of the Plantagenets.

The Pipe Rolls of 1168 record a fine of three marks imposed on Guy de Brettwide 'for his men of Sheeptor because they have dug tin in the King's forest against the rules', and 'the Lord of Brisworthy' for the same offence, was fined twenty marks, presumably because he did better than Guy. The discovery of tin may have added to the royal treasury, but it was a mixed blessing, for the Abbots of Tavistock. Tin mining was regulated by the assize of mines, and one of its impositions allowed any man, if he discovered tin, to stake out his claim on a tin lode and there work, be he lord or serf, without hindrance of any man. If he happened to be a serf, he could disregard his lord's command to work on the manor, and dig his own tin instead. By the middle of the twelfth century, the Abbot had to waive services from his serfs, probably because they were enterprising men who had discovered tin for themselves. What was he to do? If he tried to impose labour services, he would meet opposition, and risk judgement before the Royal Courts for going against the King's Writ. The Abbot solved his problem by founding the borough of Tavistock.

He set aside an area within which all tenants were to become burgesses, in other words, all his serfs became freeholders, owing only money rent, with the exception of eighteen serfs, who still owed some trifling services to the Abbey. The brain behind this scheme was probably Abbot Walter (1156-68), for his reign coincides with the dramatic expansion of the Dartmoor tin trade. As prospectors for tin were drawn towards Tavistock, the demand for houses was increased. Serfs freed from labour turned their energies to streaming, bringing their product to market in the new borough, and merchants and traders, who had formerly stopped to do business at Okehampton, now made their way to Tavistock.

Remains of the medieval 'Still House' of Tavistock Abbey, possibly originally part of the infirmary. The photograph was taken by Robert Burnard in July 1891.

Here they could buy tin, thus replenishing the Abbot's Treasury with the tolls and taxes they paid for entry to the town and trading therein.

Prosperity had come to Tavistock. In 1294 it was chosen by the Royal Assessors, along with five other Devon towns as being capable of supporting the burden of higher taxation, and by 1305, its importance as a trading centre was recognised, and it became a Stannary town.

Very different was the thirteenth century borough to the town of today. Within its boundaries were the woodlands, arable and meadowlands, weeded and worked by the original farmers of the manor. No provision had been made for an increase in population, since the new burgesses lived by trade and handicrafts. Even today, despite a recent house-building boom, a little more than half of the 325 acres set up in the original borough is at present built upon. Until 1945 corn grew beside the Launceston road on the approaches to the town, at the very spot where the thirteenth century peasants had their arable strips.

An entail of this date conjures up a picture of the developing town as a patchwork of small houses, interspersed with gardens and orchards, where numerous small foot bridges crossed the mill brook and fish lake, both of which can be seen in present day Tavistock. There was a leper hospital, which rented its own garden, whilst the needs of the townsfolk were answered by a variety of mills to which tenants were bound to go, giving a toll to the Abbot for the privilege of grinding their corn on his property.

The centres of activity were the parish church and the market place. Here in the Shambles, meat and fish were sold on market days. Here too the 'Shammel Moot' was held, presided over by the Lord's Steward so that complaints and crimes occurring in the borough might be dealt with, and the Portreeve chosen from among the burgesses, he being a man of some standing, responsible for the collection of rents and tolls within the borough.

Once Tavistock had been designated a Stannary town, the Abbots unlike many other lords on Dartmoor, gained ample compensation, for the merchants who travelled from far and near, found there an established market, with a wide variety of provisions. Unlike Chagford, on the further side of the moor, or Okehampton, goods of all kinds could be easily transported to and from the Tamar quay at Morwellham, and no doubt these buyers and sellers brought offerings to the shrine of St Rumon in the Abbey Church. The Abbot's income from rents also expanded as the population increased.

The spiritual welfare of such a flourishing community was not forgotten, and by 1180, a secular priest, one John the Chaplain, had been appointed to look after the townsfolk. Early in the thirteenth century, a new parish church was built and dedicated to St Eustace, and in 1318, not long after Tavistock became a Stannary town, this church had to be enlarged, so that by 1385 it was at least 378 feet long, and contained not less than eight altars, dedicated to the Blessed Virgin and other saints, which doubtless supplied rewards to the parish more material than spiritual.

The Abbots certainly had their sights on mundane affairs. From time to time they intervened directly in the business of mining, and in May 1319 the reigning Abbot was appointed (for ten years), Warden of Devon's Stannaries and Keeper of the Port of Dartmouth. A year later he was leasing the Exchequer revenues for £100 per annum.

But there was to be no peace for the wicked, for during the confusion brought about by the overthrow of Edward II, and the interregnum of Isabella and Mortimer, there was a series of contradictory grants to people, other than the Abbot, despite numerous petitions made by him and his monks to revoke the orders. Still more disturbing, was a disastrous vacancy prolonged over three years (1324-7), which wrecked the prosperity enjoyed by the Abbey under Robert Champeaux. This nearly lost Tavistock its title of Stannary town, for a plot was hatched by the burgesses of Plympton, who tried by devious means to have the coinage removed from Tavistock, so that their town could take its place.

'Remains of Tavistock Priory',
1820 etching by J. Coney.

But Tavistock remained a tin centre despite these difficulties. Five miles from the town the courts of justicator were held, and nearby was Crockern Tor, the ancient site of the Stannary Parliament. Indeed, the first printed copy of the Stannary Laws was made in Tavistock, on one of the oldest presses in Europe, the Caxton press in Tavistock Abbey.

Both the Tavistock Stannary Court Rolls, and some of its Coinage Rolls, exist to this day, and they help to bring to life the tinners of those distant times, ordinary people committing the same petty crimes that come up before the magistrates courts even today.

When the tinners were not digging, they were often trespassing; like Reginald Strede, caught in someone else's field of rye, or one Hillewode, indicted for stealing apples. A little further up the social scale was John Baggetor, charged with failure to pay 'venville rent'.

The end of the Middle Ages saw the end of Tavistock as a wealthy tin centre. By 1381 easily accessible deposits had been worked out in the Plym valley, and there were other blows too: the expulsion of the Jews, and the Black Death. With the failing economy of the fifteenth century the fate of the place was sealed, and the Dissolution of the Monasteries saw the end of old Tavistock. The great Abbey, which had been its heart and soul, passed away almost without a trace.

This once prosperous industrial centre had to wait another three hundred years, until the nineteenth century copper boom, before it could know again anything like the wealth and activity of the Middle Ages. Now that has gone too. Only the gaunt ruined mine chimneys on the hills, the old arches and the fragments of Abbey wall bear witness to those splendid days when merchants and pilgrims flocked to Tavistock to buy and sell their tin and to honour the bones of St Rumon, and the later times when they shipped their copper down the Tamar. The smiling sleepy town is left to its dreams and its memories with those who can enjoy its charm, while busier people hurry away to Plymouth and Cornwall.

'The South East Prospect of the Town of Tavistoke', 1741.

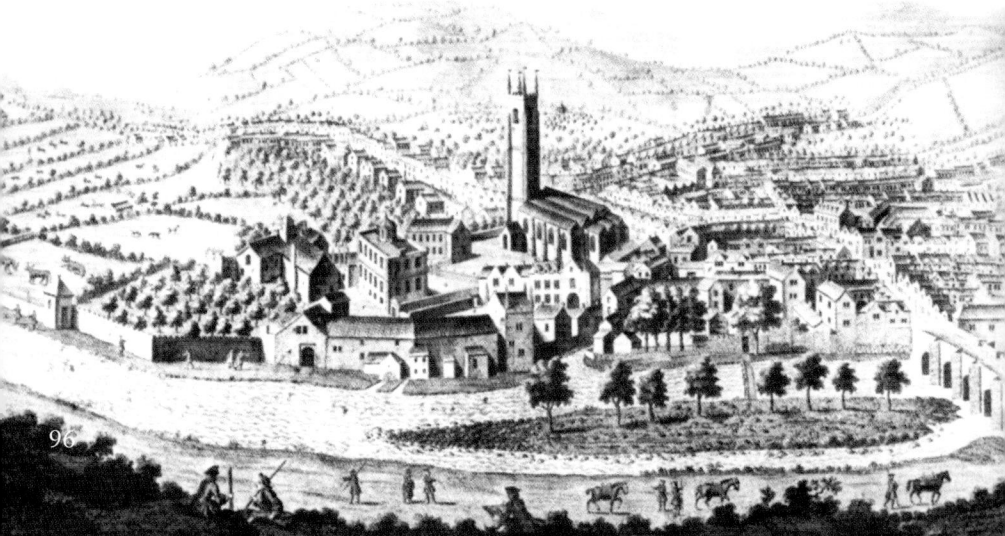

Chapter 8
Tin in the Tavistock Area

From the earliest times 'Tavistock in the moor' was linked to Plympton by a route which curved to the north-east of the deeper stretches of the Walkham and Plym valleys. Thanks to the many stone crosses which mark its way, it is still possible to follow this route with ease. Initially, the way stretches bleakly across the spectacular lunar landscape which clay working has made of Lee Moor. The hills have been cut into surrealist shapes and dazzling white spoil heaps which dominate the view for miles around. Their angular contours merge incongruously with the wider sweep of high moorland, broken occasionally by the stark outline of the high tors.

Once this wasteland was the site of Bronze Age villages. In those far off days, the climate was considerably warmer than it is today, so enabling the inhabitants to cultivate grain and to survive without much hardship. It turned colder in the Middle Ages, and during the time of the tinners, rain, mist, and snow, had made the erection of crosses a necessity for travellers using the trackways and pack-horse routes to and from the moor.

Over Shaugh Prior and on Lee Moor we can still follow them, at Beatland Corner, Shadenmoor and Blacktor they chart the route of the old track, and there is another by Cadover Bridge where the road crosses the little stream that will widen later on into the river Plym. In the Middle Ages this was a clapper bridge, mentioned in a Charter of Isabella de Fortibus (1291) as 'Ponte de Cadaworth'.

Brisworthy, situated just above the bridge, was originally a venville, or farm, dating from the days when Dartmoor was afforested (that is before the Norman Conquest) for it had certain rights on 'the forest of Dartmoor' of pasture or turbary'. There are records of the extraction of tin here in the Pipe Roll of 1156, and maybe that is when the hamlet of Brisworthy sprang up. By Norman times it must have been a busy little settlement for there was a rabbit warren at Trowlesworthy, scattered among the ruins of enclosures and hut circles on either bank of the infant Plym.

lunar landscape of Lee Moor works seen from Shell Top

All round Cadover Bridge and up the river towards Lee Moor are traces of tin streams and, at Brisworthy Burrows and Brisworthy hamlet, there are the remains of two blowing houses. The old road to Tavistock continued through Meavy, where it is marked by Marchants Cross (left), which stood there in Norman times, if not before. Quite possibly these villagers were part-time tinners, certainly the industry was in full swing here in the sixteenth century and early seventeenth century when in 1610, John Woolcombe built Yeo Farm. Stones from a blowing house can be seen incorporated in some of its out-houses, and this suggests that the old buildings used by the tinners of earlier days had fallen into disuse.

Following the river Meavy upstream, we reach the delightful village of Sheepstor, another venville farm, and also mentioned in the Pipe Rolls. It is set deep in a wooded valley, now largely inundated by Burrator Reservoir, surely one of the most beautiful artificial lakes in the country. From its placid waters, ringed by thick oak woods, rise the peaks of Sheepstor and Leathertor, while beneath the lake lie drowned farmsteads and cottages, abandoned before the encroaching waters.

When gazing down on the sleepy village and quiet lake, it gives one quite a start to remember what a hive of industry this valley was back in the Middle Ages. All round these wooded streams, Meavy, Hart Tor Brook, Newleycombe Lake and Deancombe Brook are the tell-tale signs of open tin workings, making it rough going for the present-day walker.

There was certainly a blowing house at Langstone, close to an ancient dwelling, and there are another two at Nosworthy, site of a medieval farmhouse, and at Riddipit, a few yards above Leathertor Bridge. A pair of well-preserved blowing houses lie just below Cramber Tor, on either side of Blacktor Falls. Round them lie their mortar stones; and the ruin on the east bank is particularly interesting, for its door lintel (right) inscribed 'XII' still stands, and this probably connects it with the registration of blowing houses in the reign of James I. Just below these remains are two ruined huts which may well have been used as shelters by tinners and smelters.

Below Cramber Tor, stream tin works are plainly visible among the bracken and quarrying of later days. We are by now out on the moor again, having moved

Crazywell Pool has given rise to a number of legends but its origins are thought to be the excavations of miners.

away from the medieval excavations and back into the Bronze Age. Cramber Tor is littered with cairns, hut circles and enclosures. But into the middle of this exposed landscape tin and history intrude once more, for a fascinating fragment of folklore links Crazywell Pool with Piers Gaveston, favourite of Edward II. During his exile from Court, he is said to have visited the pool to consult the oracle in its depths. Now it just so happens that this disastrous young nobleman did hold the Wardenship of the Stannaries, but the story is clearly fanciful, not least as it is unlikely that, at a time when the tin industry was flourishing (and it was booming in the thirteen hundreds), Crazywell would have been flooded, as it is now.

In the thickly wooded valley below is yet another blowing house at Deancombe on Deancombe Brook. Though small, it is easily recognisable for most of the mortar stones have been used to build a low wall two hundred yards away, and others lie beneath thick undergrowth round the site. The remaining furnace which is constructed of high boulders, is almost complete, and all round the house are the piles of sand remnants of the processing of tin ore.

On Sheepstor Brook are two more blowing houses, at Colleytown, and just below Yellowmead Farm. Though the actual buildings here vanished long ago,

Extensive tin workings at Deancombe.

mould stones and mill stones have been found in and around the little farm, to one side of which numerous tin workings may be seen. There is an ancient stone circle on the opposite bank, and from here to Sheepstor Bridge runs an ancient track which continues to the Tavistock road.

This route now crosses the rolling splendour of Walkhampton Common where lofty, desolate tors rise, square and massive, like the ruins of an ancient stronghold, and through this granite landscape flows the river Walkham. Its course from Merrivale and northern Dartmoor takes it under Horrabridge and through the beautiful leafy valley from which rise Pew Tor and Vixen Tor, high above. At Merrivale it is crossed by the track from Chagford at a bridge that was recorded in the fifteenth century, and was probably in use long before that time. Beyond Merrivale the old road into Tavistock, which lay south of the present one, ran by Windy Post and Moortown and over Whitchurch Down. Dropping steeply to the Tavy, it crosses this river by the Great Bridge, which was probably first built in 1260.

The present settlement at Merrivale results from the granite quarry, opened in 1876, and whose massive spoil heaps overlook the old tin streamworks, of which there are three very near the road.

Kit Mine, also known as Sheepstor Tin Mine, was worked for around a century from the early 1800s. These stamps, used for crushing ore, date from the later years of the mine's operation and were photographed in 1933, three years before they were removed and sold for scrap.

Merrivale c.1910 looking over the old road bridge spanning the Walkham towards the quarry.

Chapter 9
Plympton: Birth of a Great Port

So here we are at Plympton, off the moor, and close to the coast. Ashburton, Chagford and Tavistock had been holding their coinages for many a year, before Plympton became a Stannary town, but it had been playing its part for centuries in the history of the tinners and its own tale is fascinating, its history entwined with Plymouth's: the child which took over its parent, a bacon quay that became a world famous port! Dartmoor historian Samuel Rowe repeated the famous rhyme: 'Plympton was a borough town, when Plymouth was a furzy down', when writing about the place.

In the time of the Romans the Plym estuary was navigable right up to its head, and there was a trading settlement at what is now Mount Batten. It was only a little place, and it faded out in the Dark Ages, but coins have been found that substantiate the Roman presence.

Recorded as 'Plymentum' in Saxon times, it boasted a Collegiate Church with a timbered minster of which there is no longer any trace. There was a tiny settlement at Sutton and a much larger one at Stoke. Nearby was the royal estate of Kings Tamerton.

It is with the Normans that the story of Plympton really begins, for the Conqueror's nephew, William Warelwast, founded the Augustinian Priory at Plympton St Mary and his cousin Baldwin de Redvers built the castle at Plympton Earl. The Normans divided Plympton in half, and so it has remained ever since.

Plympton Castle and St Maurice church, William Payne c.1800.

A map of Plymouth and surrounding area c.1500 showing how the rivers then provided passage much farther inland than was possible later. Plympton, which was easily navigable from the sea, is shown on the far right of the map at A, at the confluence of the rivers Plym and Meavy. Ironically it was the silting up of these rivers in large part due to mining activities on the moor that eventually put an end to Plympton's prominence.

The stories of the Devon Stannaries are each intriguingly different. Ashburton, the royal manor and trading centre, has an international flavour; Chagford's is a tale of everyday people, living and working in the feudal countryside and Tavistock's history is dominated by the great Abbey. Plympton had its Priory too, but there were also two great families who called the tune, overseeing the little port that grew and grew until it swamped everything else.

Thanks to the invaluable Domesday Survey (1086), we know a great deal about Norman Plympton, and because of its 'double identity' there was a double survey too, the Exchequer Book, and the Exeter Book (now in Exeter Cathedral Library). This book tells us that the King's Manor called Plintona comprised 2½ hides. It continues with a list of ploughs, villeins, serfs, cattle, sheep, timber and pasture, and ends 'when Baldwin received it, it rendered £12 10s'. The Canons of St Peter, Exeter, had 2 hides worth 35s. Quite a difference! The Exchequer Survey exactly confirms these statistics.

Plympton Castle ruins.

The two parts of Plympton are now known as St Mary and St Maurice from the dedication of the two churches, but in the early days, St Maurice, the more important of the twins, was called Plympton Earl, because it was held by the de Redvers family whose earldom was created by Henry I. The ruins of de Redvers' castle are not far from St Maurice's church, surrounded by a bank and a ditch, probably thrown up in Saxon times as a place of cover from the Danes. We do not know whether it was originally a natural mound, but it had certainly been used by the valley community as a prepared refuge in case of emergency. Baldwin de Redvers strengthened it as an outpost, guarding his Devon estates, and his son, Richard, built the keep on the site of the earlier timbered structure, but as the motte was never strong enough for a heavy stone fort, it remained a light construction, surrounded by a moat, which could be defended if the bailey fell.

The castle had a short and inglorious history but its remains are still with us. The Priory, founded in 1121, lasted four hundred years to vanish almost without a trace. Of its library, only one book remains, a transcript of Bede's *History of the English Church*, a fine example of a twelfth century manuscript. On its back pages the Canons kept a rough chronicle of national and other events. An entry of 1121 tells of the foundation of the Priory, a further one of the last days of Bishop Warelwast, who on his retirement from public life, took the habit of an Austin Canon at Plympton and died there in 1137.

The old Collegiate Church had been swept away by the Normans, and the small number of secular clergy to whom it was home were, according to Leland 'displaced because they would not leave their concubines', which probably means that they were married and refused the vow of celibacy. They were removed by the Bishop to the College of Bosham and presumably the concubines went too. They certainly would not have hit it off with the distinctly 'upper class' Austin Canons, who considering themselves superior intellectually, employed servants to do the dirty work, and concentrated on estate management and the production of manuscripts. They multiplied thick and fast after the Conquest, and the

From Here to There

'They have few wheeled carriages by reason of the steep hills, but everything is carried on hooks each side of the horses.'

Dr Richard Pococke 1750.

In some quarters is has been suggested that wheeled transport came late to Dartmoor as though signifying the backward nature of its people. The simple truth is that the moorland terrain, steep, strewn with rocks, and awash with streams and mires, made wheeled transport far less practicable than pack-saddles and drags (sledges). For the early tin miners, especially those on the more remote parts of the moor the pony and pack-saddle provided the best means of moving tools, materials and tin ingots readily and safely.

Thomas Rowlandson depicted the use of the sledge or 'drag' in his watercolour 'Bringing Home Timber, Devonshire' c.1800. William Marshall, writing about Dartmoor in 1796, records 'the dray or sledge is found in the lowest rank of simplicity. Merely two side pieces joined together by cross bars. It is large, strong and useful on many occasions.' That the use of the sledge survived well into the late 1800s is shown in this photograph from the Hunt Collection taken at Foxworthy Farm in Lustleigh.

While clapper bridges served well for crossing streams on the high moor they were precarious even for travellers on foot and subject to being washed away in storms. Wherever practicable, clappers were replaced by arched bridges, often just wide enough for two pack-horse trains to pass each other. Rowlandson's painting depicts the scene in Devon c.1800, the man in charge of the train paying the toll due for crossing the bridge.

Below left: Hisley pack-horse bridge crosses the River Bovey between Lustligh and Manaton parishes. It is typical of many such bridges on and around the moor.

A pack-saddle photographed at Foxworthy around 1900. By this time, roads improved, the saddle was seen as an object of curiosity rather than as purely functional.

The pack-saddle, while simple in its construction was extremely versatile in its use, depending upon the load to be carried. In his book The Old Devon Farmhouse, Peter Brears illustrates a variety of crooks and pots which could be attached to the saddle depending upon the type of load. Marshall suggests the use of bags slung over the saddle for the carriage of stones or sand and perhaps this is what miners used when transporting tin ore any distance.

King Stephen.

Bodmin and Launceston Priories were also founded by Bishop Warelwast, though Plympton was always his favourite.

But when they laid the old man to rest in the Chapter House, the King under whom so much had been achieved, had been dead two years, and the peace of his reign had given place to the turmoil of Stephen. Baldwin II was now Lord of Plympton Earl and he sided with Matilda. Ordering his men at arms to defend Plympton, he marched off to the siege of Exeter, and never returned.

Left to themselves the garrison behaved quite deplorably. When Stephen arrived, they took one look from the battlements and promptly surrendered. The King stripped the castle of everything, reduced the fortifications to ruins and drove off the sheep and cattle. It was never rebuilt.

Matilda.

A survey of the Barony of Plympton shortly after the death of Isabella de Fortibus states 'that tenants were bound to keep up the wall and battlements at their own cost, and the Lord, the moat and tower', which sounds very grand, but a manuscript of 1481 hints at a somewhat undignified use for the moat, for it relates that a ducking stool was situated 'in the old castle ditch'!

With the advent of Henry II, Plympton settled down to a pattern of life which was to continue for the next three hundred years. Indeed 'the extensive prospect' was much the same when the Revd Samuel Rowe, standing on the old hill fort known as Boringdon Camp, gazing across the valley, could plainly discern Plymouth Sound at a distance of seven miles to the south-west. In this lovely fertile valley lay the thirteen de Redvers' manors, all, except one, surviving to this day as farms and country houses. Four more famous houses originated in the reigns of the first two Plantagenets, Sparkwell (1167), Saltram and Boringdon later homes of the Parker family (1249 and 1279), and Newnham, seat of the Strodes in 1292. The Canons held the hides of Boringdon and Wembury. Here through the centuries the feudal tenants pursued the agricultural cycle, sowing, reaping and paying their dues.

However, the estuary was slowly silting up, and though Devon slates were still shipped to Southampton from Plympton late in the twelfth century, it soon ceased to be a port, and shipping began to move to the Canon's quay at Sutton. When, in 1211, a cargo of bacon was carried to Portsmouth from Plymouth, the smaller ports were quickly overshadowed and a great port had been born.

It was, however, a slow starter, for Plymouth's situation was far to the west of the country and it lay wide open to the south-west gales. Also the new town springing up round Sutton Quay was always at loggerheads with the Priory. In those days the principal Devon port was the sheltered harbour of Dartmouth, here the European fleet of the Second Crusade assembled as did King John's invasion of Poitou. With the advent of the Angevins the western Channel ports had become strategically important. Of the two, Dartmouth was less vulnerable to French raiders than Plymouth. Even so, there was loot at Sutton worth taking, for the humble bacon cargoes had given place to tin.

Though Plympton did not become a Stannary town until 1328, the area, 'a wedge of land adjoining Plymouth on the west and bounded on the east by a line from Crockern Tor through Modbury to Burgh Island' was being worked hard by the streamers. And, as we saw in the preceding chapter, the Burrator area, so rich in blowing houses is no distance away. On the northern boundaries of Plympton, along the ridge and into Newnham Park, the tinners' workings are plainly to be seen. In Fernhill Wood are scores of scattered pits of considerable depths, while long trenches (coffins) indicate the line of the main lode.

Following the twelfth century Charter, the tinners, set free from manorial restrictions, and strengthened by their right under the Stannary Laws to search for tin on Manor land, and carry their water to their works, turned gladly from agriculture, and began to dig all over the area, to the inevitable annoyance of everybody else. They did a great deal of damage to agricultural land by directing streams, and sluicing out trenches with running water. When Leland visited the old Priory in the sixteenth century, he noticed that even its grounds were silted up with red sand, brought down the Tory Brook from the tin works.

With the tinners went their rabbits, and the warreners of the Plym Valley found a good market in Plymouth, a trade which continued for hundreds of years well into the railway era when Plym rabbits were being sent all over England.

Every week there was a tin court at Plympton Earl, frequented by tinners from the Tavistock Stannary as well as the local men, where business was handled and recorded in Rolls resembling those of a Manor Court. Larger trading took place at the coinage at Ashburton, but soon Plympton itself was to become a Stannary town, for it was now a place of considerable importance, having, in 1194, been created a Borough.

This meant that the Lord, in this case William de Redvers, Earl of Devon, contented himself with a money rent from the inhabitants and claimed few or none of the manorial services which he got from his rural tenants; burgage tenure being a form of freehold.

Plympton was granted a Charter in 1242 and, from that day until 1859, it boasted a Mayor and Corporation. In 1294 it was taxed as one of the six most important towns in Devon. It sent two burgesses to Parliament at Westminster, and it boasted four churches.

Arms of William de Redvers 5th Earl of Devon.

One of these was, of course, the Priory which has completely disappeared as has the Maudlyn Leper Hospital which used to stand in Higher Ridgeway (now Elm Terrace). The other two are the parish church of St Mary 'for the perpetual finding of a priest and main divine service at the Chapel called St Morris'. This church, St Maurice of Plympton Earl, now stands among a cluster of charming Georgian houses not far from the ruins of the castle, its imposing tower being visible from quite a distance. It appears to have started life as a chapel served by the Priory, and it would be interesting to know how it came by its unusual dedication. We do know that Henry VIII forbid the veneration of Thomas Becket and that the dedication was this quickly changed from Thomas to Maurice. In his book *English Church Dedications*, Nicholas Orme writes 'one wonders why Maurice, who though not a cleric, had suffered for the faith under an earlier ruler. Was this covert defiance?' In other words by choosing Maurice, Plymptonians were showing the same independent spirit found among their tinning brethren.

A visit to the church is well worth the trouble. It is a charming perpendicular structure, beautifully cared for, with a little chapel (dedicated to the original Theban martyr), memorial to the generosity of John Brackley, Member of Parliament in 1382.

The Revd Samuel Rowe has plenty to say about the siting of this church 'in a situation which originally must have been little better than a marsh'. It lies quite a distance from Plympton Earl (the former Borough) right by the site of the Priory. In fact remains of the Priory church were discovered in 1950 in a garden just south of the churchyard. Rowe accounts for this by recounting a legend of the miraculous removal of building materials from the original site near the castle to the present one by 'the Enemy' (i.e. the Devil). In this case he did Plympton a good turn. Had he not done so, St Maurice would have two churches cheek by jowl, and St Mary's no church at all.

Plymouth at this time had only the little chapel of St Andrew, but it was growing in size and importance, and in 1253 the Prior obtained from the King the right to hold a weekly market and a three-day annual fair. But he refused to allow the growing port a mayor and appointed his own bailiff. In 1298 however, it had sprung into national prominence and was sending two Members to Parliament.

Blackaton (Romans) Cross was a way-marker on the route across the moor to Plympton Priory from Tavistock. These ancient crosses would have provided familiar landmarks to tinners making their way to the Stannary towns.

In 1294, war had broken out between Edward I and Philip IV of France, and a furious quarrel ensued between the King, on the one hand, and the church and barons on the other, over taxation. King Edward promptly removed himself from Westminster to Plympton Priory. He stayed there conducting the affairs of the Kingdom (and the Canons) from April 10th to June 18th and nearly ruining them in the process. In 1910, a coin of Edward I was unearthed on the site of the Priory, memento of those two months when Plympton was the capital of England.

Sixty years later they had another visitation, this time from the Black Prince, conducting affairs of the Duchy, while contrary winds delayed his Gascony-bound fleet at Plymouth. And in November, 1362, he was back again for a fortnight. Small wonder that the Canons complained that they were beggared by their illustrious guests.

The trouble was that they were not sufficiently 'off the road' and now that Plympton Earl was a thriving Borough people were flocking to its markets and fairs. There was a busy trade in local products, an expanding industry in wool and cloth, and now a tin boom, and a growing port from which to export it. Access was also good, there was a highway from Exeter to Plymouth, which was joined by the main route across the moor somewhere near the Priory. The result was that all sorts of people arrived there, expecting hospitality, and usually getting it. In 1261, the Bishop gave the Canons leave to appropriate Dean Prior 'to relieve the necessities of poor wayfaring men' and, in 1338, they got the revenues of Newton St Cyres as well. It was not only for the needs of wayfarers that they needed the money, for in 1328 Plympton became a Stannary town, thanks to the great family who had now succeeded to the Lordship.

We have referred several times in the course of this story to Isabella de Fortibus. She was the last of the de Redvers and she outlived all her family, dying in 1293. The succession passed by devious ways to Lord Hugh Courtenay, whose family had come to England with Eleanor of Aquitaine. He was a very powerful man, who united the honour of Plympton with that of Okehampton, and in 1335 he was created Earl of Devon. In 1328 he had taken advantage of trouble at Tavistock Abbey, and the fact that, owing to its distance from the sea, less and less tin was being coined at Tavistock, whilst more and more was being shipped from Plymouth, to bring his influence to bear on the new King, Edward III, to get Plympton substituted for Tavistock as a Stannary town. Later Tavistock was reinstated; but Plympton retained its tin court and market for the duration of surface mining, though it must be admitted that statistics show it to be the least important of the four Stannaries. Its new status however, not to speak of the growth of Plymouth, brought more and more travellers to take advantage of open house at the Priory.

Their revenues should have been sufficient to support them, for they had assets all over the country. They also had their own Grange (farmstead), with its Bailiff in Priory livery. The ancient building at Higher Ridgeway called Grange was probably the monastic barn.

But there were disasters. Among the Stannary Papers (lost in an air raid in 1941) mention was made of 'houses fully drowned and no rent received'. When this flood occurred we do not know, for there is no date. Of course the Black

Rebels & Revolution

Detail from John Hooker's map of Exeter, 1587. No stranger to sieges, walled towns were a prime target for rebel armies for capturing them would mean gaining a strategic stronghold.

The natural independence of early miners, their special protection under Stannary Law, created a strength of community among them. This, combined with their tough and often solitary working conditions, created a breed of men that it was unwise to provoke. It is recorded earlier how, in 1494, Richard Strode endured a brief spell in Lydford gaol for incurring the wrath of the Devon tinners.

The Cornish Rebellion of 1497 originated among the miners who opposed Henry VII's raising of taxes to promote his war against Scotland. While Devon miners had earlier accepted changes to the Stannary Law which meant they escaped the higher tax being imposed, a number of Devon men joined the ill-fated rebel march on London, besieging Exeter on the way.

In 1549, during what became known as the Prayer Book Rebellion, or Western Rising, Exeter again came under siege, with miners on both sides figuring in events. Cornish miners in the 2000-strong rebel force were engaged to use their knowledge of explosives to breach the city walls, while inside the city, a Devon miner, John Newcombe of Teignmouth, was called upon to thwart their plans by organising the digging of countermines and the flooding of the rebels' tunnels:

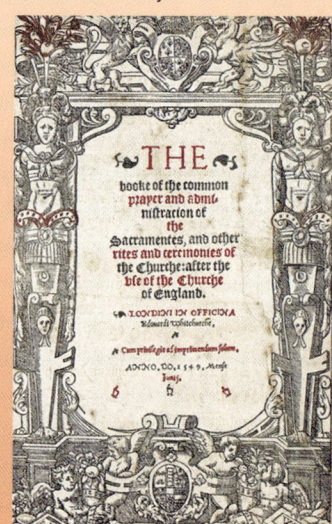

Frontispiece to The Book of Common Prayer, *1549, the introduction of which sparked unrest among Catholics objecting to the theology of the English Reformation.*

> *Understanding the designs of the enemy, he said he would endeavour to frustrate their scheme; which he effected in this manner: hearing a noise under ground, he takes a pan of water, and by removing it from place to place, came at length to the very spot where the miners were working; which he knew for certain by the shaking of the water in the pan. Immediately on this discovery he set about countermining them; which he did to so good purpose, that in a little time he could and actually did look into their workings. He then caused every inhabitant who lived in any of the streets that had a fall or descent into the said West Gate, to place at his fore-*

door a great tub or tubs filled with water, and all the wells and tirpits in these streets to be drawn off, and emptied at one and the same instant that the tubs of water were overset; which running in great abundance towards the said gate, was presently conveyed to the place counter-mined, and there entered the places first mined. The great goodness of God was also further to be observed and admired upon this occasion; for just at the time that the wells were draining off, there fell so great a shower of rain, that, (for the time it lasted) the like had not been remembered for many years.

Also within the city lived 'a tinner of Chagford named Kingwell', who was called upon to act as a courier conveying a secret message from his master, John Charles of Tavistock, to Lord Russell who commanded the King's forces. While attempting to evade the besiegers Kingwell is captured and, at first, the rebels attempt to persuade him to join them:

John Russell, Lord Privy Seal, was ordered by Edward VI to quell the rebels, a task which he undertook with the help of a mercenary army.

> They used all the devices they could to recover him to their opinions, sometimes fair words sometimes with threatenings and sometimes with imprisonments: but still he inveighed against them calling them rebels and traitors both against God and the King. Such a fire-brand and encourager of mutiny could not be allowed to continue in these evil courses, and, all other means failing to reclaim him to their disposition he was taken out of prison and forthwith condemned to be hanged.

Popular rebellions were not uncommon in the fifteenth and sixteenth centuries in Europe, and while those who made up the Cornish and Devon rebel army were obliged to undertake regular military training, their 7000 strong force was no match for the 8600 mercenary-led army organised by Lord Russell which, in a series of bloody battles, eventually defeated the rebels at Sampford Courtenay. The left hand picture shows a rebel force armed largely with pikes and pitchforks, the mercenary (right) is a professional soldier armed with the latest weaponry.

Death affected everybody's revenues, and that was the year after the Black Prince's visit. So they were always in debt, and, as a result, they kept up running fights with Plymouth (which was trying, and failing, to become independent of the Prior), and with the unfortunate Maudlyn Hospital over the allowance of food for its inmates. As a result the Priory appears to have made itself distinctly unpopular, and perhaps this was the cause of an intriguing anecdote which appears in an undated document.

'Prior Robert in a parliamentary petition complained of serious rioting'. One of his servants had died and was buried at St Mary's. Nine days later an armed mob of townsfolk led by one John Sylverlock burst into the church, dug up the corpse, and horribly mishandled it. The dead man had probably been the Prior's tax collector, for they appear to have held a macabre offertory in the churchyard and then made their way to the local alehouse with the proceeds. They drank heavily and trooped out again to lie in wait for anyone emerging from the Priory. They did set upon an unfortunate Canon who arrived to say Mass, and who only saved himself by taking refuge in the vestry, and in consequence the Prior and Canons were prevented from saying Mass in St Mary's, its doors being closed against them. 'They dared not come forth but went in fear of their lives,' but how it all ended we do not know, for the rest is lost.

Standing in the lawn-like churchyard of St Mary, beneath its great hundred foot granite tower, it is not easy to visualize these stirring events. The interior of the church, dating principally from the fourteenth and fifteenth centuries, and, built of granite, is a fine, spacious example of its period, though somewhat cold and dark. It boasts some ancient heraldic glass, and a handsome sedile and piscina in the chancel. But by far its most notable features are its magnificent tombs, the most remarkable being that of Richard Strode in full armour.

Plympton St Mary church, a watercolour by Revd John Swete, 1797.

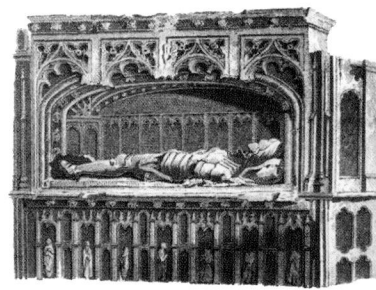

Richard Strode's tomb in St Mary's church, Plympton.

The tower is embattled, pinnacled and crocketted and the north and south porticoes are also embattled. As the main part of this building was constructed from the profits of the tin industry, after the Black Death, we can only conclude that this tragedy, which resulted in a considerable fall in the population, cannot have affected the prosperity of Plympton.

People were still flocking into St Mary's for the Midsummer Fair, and to Plympton Earl for the market which was held in the main street, and contemporary documents prove that the inhabitants enjoyed a comfortable standard of living. The Stannary of Plympton was doing well under the Courtenays.

Plymouth too was expanding, catching up and passing Dartmouth, but it had its ups and downs. In 1403 a considerable force of Bretons raided the town and burnt a number of houses, and it took the young port a long time to recover. To this day, the site of the disaster is called Bretonside.

However, in 1439, Henry VI agreed that the three Suttons should be amalgamated into a single town of Plymouth, under a Mayor and Corporation. They were free at last of the Priory, and their first Mayor was appointed in 1440. Had Hull not beaten them by a few months, they would have been the first town in England to be thus incorporated. Their disputes with the Priory continued, and they were badly hit by poor trade and the depression of the fifteenth century. Despite this, however, and thanks to a benefactor, Thomas Yogge, the main part of St Andrew's parish church was built, and the tower erected.

Now it was that disaster came to the Courtenays. Connected by marriage to the Lancastrian Royal House, four of them died violently for the Red Rose, and though Sir Hugh Courtenay of Haccombe was raised to the Earldom of Devon by Henry VII, he again made the fatal mistake of marrying into the Royal Family, thus bringing grief and dissolution to his descendants.

What Plympton Earl thought of it all, as the Lordship battled to and fro, we are not told, for they were happily far from the scene of action. It was the affairs of another family which interested them, a solid reliable Devon family, Strode of Newnham.

Old Newnham Farm House stands at the east end of the Colebrook Valley where the road divides from that to Lee Moor. The present house was built in 1700, but there are traces of the Tudor mansion built by the Strodes on the site of the old manor of Simon de Plympton, which they inherited by marriage in the early fifteenth century. The grandson of this marriage, Richard, Member of Parliament for Plympton, is the splendid warrior, who lies in St Katherine's Chapel of Plympton St Mary. He was adamant in his will as to where this tomb should be. Did he choose St Katherine's Chapel because he was a tin owner?

These were good times for the 'Gentlemen Tinners', who were becoming very interested in the profits of the industry. About the mid-fifteenth century they

'Old Nuneham House' by Revd John Swete 1797, original home of the Strode family before the construction of the family's new seat at Newnham, built in the late eighteenth century.

began to strike up partnerships with the 'Labouring Tinners', and this probably suited the latter. Previously they had entered, when and where they pleased, dug tin, and handed back a share of it. Now the days of feudalism were drawing to a close, and it was better all round, to make peaceful arrangements. The tinners' families were often ordinary tenants of the manor, and if things got out of hand it could be awkward for them. Besides the tinners themselves were often short of money, for they could only sell four times a year at the coinages, and they were glad of the opportunity to sell at other times to the local tin dealers, who were ready to make advances, though probably at lower than coinage prices. It suited them well to go to the local gentry, work out and register pitches at the tin court, and share their profits with the landowners. As the sixteenth century dawned, this was becoming the usual practice and it led to the famous Strode Case of 1512.

We have met Richard Strode before, complaining bitterly of his experiences inside Lydford Castle. He was the grandson of Richard whose tomb stands in St Mary's, and the most famous of all Plympton's Members of Parliament. No history of the Stannaries is complete without him, for he managed to infuriate the tinners by apparently running with the hare and hunting with the hounds. Though he was himself a tinner, he introduced into Parliament a bill dealing with 'the perishing, hurting and destroying of rivers, portes, havens and crekes in the county of Devon', by the tinners' silt.

We have earlier described how they sentenced him on Crockern Tor, and had him seized by their agents, and dragged to the Stannary prison. Having languished in Lydford for three weeks, he gave his bond of £100 to the Deputy Warden and, having been freed, rushed to Westminster to pour out his woes to a sympathetic Parliament. He demanded that he be released from obligation to pay his fine, and that action be 'taken to restrain the tinners from vexing and molesting him further'. The act which was passed upholding this appeal is often quoted as the first Statement of Members' Privilege. He lived on until 1551, but it's doubtful if he was ever a very popular figure in the neighbourhood.

Tin was still being mined successfully in the area during the early years of the sixteenth century; and in 1523 the Earl of Devon himself had three hundredweight coined at Plympton. But in 1536 he died on the scaffold, the last of the two great families who had held Plympton Earl since the Conquest.

A year previously the Priory had gone, suppressed with the other great monasteries, so now the Canons really had something to grumble about. Their four hundred year reign had ended, and now their house has disappeared almost without a trace.

Everything was changing for the worse for Plympton, and for the better for Plymouth, the great port. St Maurice still retains an old world charm, and curiously the connection with a great family is there too, through Saltram House, once the seat of the Parkers and now in the hands of the National Trust. But poor St Mary has lost everything except its church.

Detail from William Payne's watercolour of Plympton St Maurice and Castle c.1790.

Mayhem & Murder

The license afforded to miners under Stannary Law gave them status but also brought opprobrium where their workings interfered with the livelihood of others. From the 12th century onwards there are recorded complaints about tinners diverting leats and waterways and, more seriously, that the streaming undertaken on the moor was creating so much debris that it was threatening to silt up major ports and harbours. Such a complaint was what landed Richard Strode in Lydford gaol, but the problem lasted for centuries both on and off the moor. However, by the end of the 18th century the case for recognising Stannary Law was increasingly under question as William Marshall, in 1796, proposes:

> The stannary laws, if any such laws can really be said to exist, ought to be forthwith abrogated, and some rational regulations be imposed; such as common men may understand, and under which industry may be protected from the rapine of adventurers.

The rebellious nature of the miner in the 15th and 16th centuries is recorded elsewhere in this book, but unruly behaviour continued. In 1796, a party of miners from Vitifer mine, enraged by the arrest of some of their colleagues for smashing windows in the town, descended upon Chagford with the intention of creating further damage. Ringing the church bells summoned locals who chased the miners and arrested them – their fate being sentenced to serve in His Majesty's navy.

Chagford had experienced a greater catastrophe on 6 March 1617 with the collapse of the Stannary Court House in which nine people were killed. Contemporary accounts put the tragedy down to a blasphemous plaintiff at court who called down God's wrath on his head should he be found to be lying.

> No sooner were the words out of his mouth when the timber and walls of the building simply collapsed, killing many people and injuring 17 more with broken limbs, bruised heads and backs. Certain of the esquires and gentlemen were killed and their limbs almost beaten to pieces.

Yet apparently amid the rubble and the bodies a small child was found alive and unhurt.

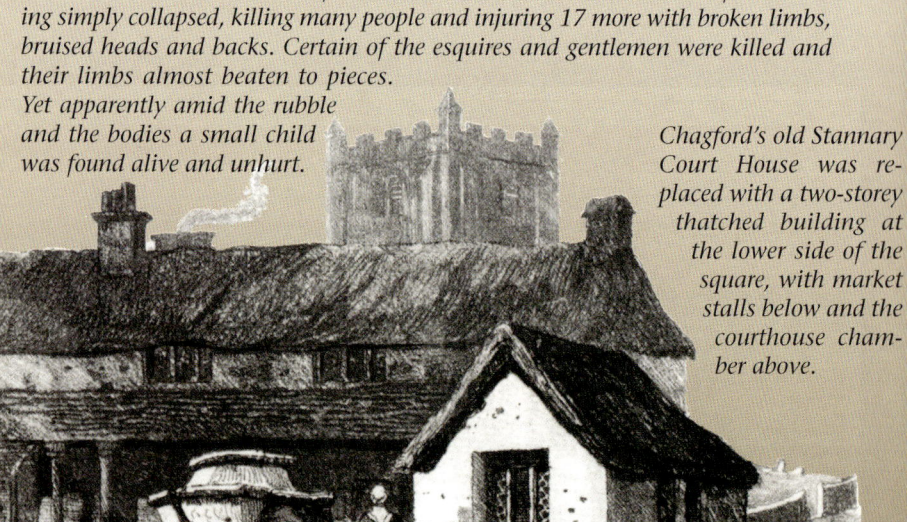

Chagford's old Stannary Court House was replaced with a two-storey thatched building at the lower side of the square, with market stalls below and the courthouse chamber above.

Nor was death far from many in the mining business for both streaming and later shaft mining held their own dangers and with medical help being scant, if available at all, the chances of surviving a major accident were slim. Coroner's Reports from the middle of the nineteenth century record a number of fatalities associated with mining:

March 1865. An Inquest was held at Mary Tavy, on Monday, by H. A. Vallack, Esq., on the body of THOMAS ROUNDSLEY, a miner, who was killed at Wheal Friendship Mine, on the previous Saturday. The deceased was at work in the shaft, and in consequence of his foot slipping from his standing place, he fell to the bottom, where he was found quite dead.

And mines were not only a danger to those working in them:

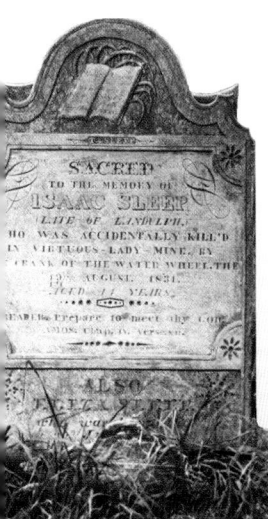

memorial in Whitchurch graveyard for Isaac Sleep who was killed by the water wheel backshaft at the Virtuous Lady Mine in 1831.

On Saturday an Inquest was held before Mr A. B. Bone, County Coroner, on the body of BENJAMIN HOLE, who was killed by falling into a mine shaft on Whitchurch Down on his return from the Tavistock races on Tuesday week. The deceased is a young man about thirty years of age and leaves a wife and four children totally unprovided for.

Few miners made their fortunes but there are recorded occasions when miners were prosecuted for selling 'uncoigned' tin, avoiding tax. No doubt those involved in associated industries, such a pewter ware, would not be averse to buying tin 'under the counter' and the enterprising tinner might always have enough spare coppers to spend an evening at an inn. For others, being in possession of money spelled danger, even death:

On St Valentine's Day 1829 James Jeffrey, Foreman of the Bottle Hill Mine, met up with two fellow miners at the Devonshire Arms in Plympton to settle some accounts. Overhearing their talk were Thomas Helston and William Trethew who hatched a plan to rob the unsuspecting Jeffrey. Although they had already arranged their lodgings for the night, they left the Devonshire Arms early, and instead asked the landlord of the George Inn if they could sleep in his hay-loft. From here they could gain direct access to and from the road, unseen by anyone at the inn. As Jeffrey made his way home he caught up with two men about a mile and a half from Ridgeway and they asked him what his business had been at the public house. Jeffrey replied, 'Nothing. It was only a gang of miners dividing their money.' Helston, then hit Jeffrey on the head with the shovel he was carrying, killing him.

Chapter 10
The Photographic Heritage

The original text of this book told the story of the early tinners on Dartmoor, the laws that brought them together and controlled them, the places they worked and the methods they used to discover tin. Stannary Law and the four towns which flourished under that law grew less significant towards the end of the 18th century, and with their end so also came the demise of the individual tin streamer, to be replaced by corporate mining companies. They brought new methods to mining on Dartmoor, the technicological development of steam pumps allowing shafts to be driven to recover metal ore from underground seams. This later story is well told elsewhere and a list of such books to help the reader is included in the bibliography.

As walking the moor becomes more popular so people are coming across the many remains of the early tinners. There follows a further selection of photographs that may help to provide some clues as to what these features are, along with photographs of some of the later mining structures and sites associated with mining, not only tin, but other minerals. The reader should be reminded again that many of these places are on private land and not accessible to the public. Mined areas still pose dangers and care must be taken in this respect.

Crockern Tor.

Above: Morwellham Quay c.1900. By this time the port was in decline but it had earlier served vessels of up to 200 tons sailing via Plymouth on the River Tamar and taking ore from the local copper mines such a Wheal Friendship which had opened in the 1790s. Ore was carried to the quay via the Tavistock canal (right), opened in 1817. The last tin coinage in Devon was held at Morwellham in 1838. The quay (below) is now part of the West Devon Mining World Heritage Site and is an educational centre and tourist attraction.

Left: What the whole thing was about. Tin ore (cassiterite) is found in many forms and required a variety of techniques in recovering it from stream beds, open cast or shaft mining. For the tin streamers the ore had already undergone a sort of refinement while being washed from the original lode and deposited along stream beds.

Below left: 'Ancient tools found at Hexworthy' is Burnard's caption to his 1890s photograph of a variety of 'gads' (short chisel-like tools used in splitting rocks), with IV being a 'modern' version for comparison.

Below right: Mr Scott demonstrates the use of a 'vanning' shovel – a photograph by R.H. Worth c.1930. These shovels were an essential tool for the streamers as they were used to assay the concentration of ore within a given sample. This was done by 'trialling' a handful of material on the blade of the shovel and by 'vanning' it (making a kind of upward flicking motion), so the heavier metallic particles were left in the centre of the shallow blade. This technique had existed from at least the 16th Century.

The Finch Foundry in Sticklepath, now a museum, manufactured tools for the mining industry.

There is little information relating to the daily life of the early tin streamers. We can assume however that, being drawn largely from the labouring classes, the tools they used and the clothes they wore were much the same as those seen on farms and in quarries, including shovels, picks and so on. Specialist tools such as the vanning shovel developed as tin mining became more specialised.

In the same way, as the industrialisation of mining increased, so what the miner wore also became more standardised, though on Dartmoor early twentieth century photographs show a motley variation in the dress code, as the Chapman postcard of miners at the entrance to Golden Dagger mine (below) shows.

Left: We know there had long been movement of miners across the border between Devon and Cornwall, the Cornish names of many of the miners (William Trethew, Thomas Johns, Richard Jory etc.) working on Dartmoor being an obvious clue to this migration. The figure on the left is a Cornish miner photographed in the late nineteenth century. He is dressed typically for the time, a heavy topcoat, stout boots and a felt hat impregnated with resin to harden it and protect the wearer's head. A candle is held at the side of the hat with a ball of clay, while he carries spare candles around his neck. At his side is a coil of safety fuse.

The early tin streamers spent much of their working lives knee deep in water as they dug through the tin-rich stream beds in Dartmoor's valleys. Later, the larger industrial mining operations provided accommodation for the miners in the form of barracks. Another innovation was the miners' dry, a building where, between shifts, the miners could shelter from the weather, eat their croust, and hope to get their working clothes dry. Richard Perryman of Manaton, who worked at Golden Dagger mine in the 1920s recalled how he was constantly wet throughout the week, drying out only when he returned home at weekends. This is the dry at Mary Tavy, seen here in a ruinous state although at one time the Dartmoor Trust had hoped to restore the building under the aegis of the Dartmoor National Park Authority. The building operated in much the same way as a Roman hypocaust with a chimney at one end and a fireplace at the other, with a flue carrying the hot draught under the raised stone floor. The dry is on private land and not open to the public.

Elsewhere the miners sought refuge in local inns. They were often not salubrious places, some offering little more than a seat by the fire and a jug of ale or cider. This is the Miners Arms at Hemerdon, seen in the 1930s when a Mr Honey was then landlord.

Burnard's photograph of the original Forest Inn at Hexworthy, taken in October 1888. This was one of two inns here serving the miners and their families. In 1900, William Crossing writes about the link between inns and the miners:

> "About twelve years ago a mine was opened near Hexworthy, on the site of some old workings, and for a time yielded tin of excellent quality. But it shared the fate of too many of the Dartmoor ventures, and after some years was closed. Recently, however, it has been reopened, and that, and Golden Dagger, near Post Bridge, are the only mines now at work on the Moor At certain periods during the last century large numbers of men must have found employment in the Dartmoor mines, and in more than one spot there were doubtless busy scenes. At all events it would appear as though such were the case, when we find that Hexworthy, which consists principally of a few farmhouses, once provided sufficient custom to support two houses of entertainment. At Headland, where there was nothing but a solitary warren, there was also an inn."

The Warren House Inn served miners from the mines nearby, including Vitifer and Golden Dagger. Watercolour by W.H. Jones c.1920.

Above: An aerial photograph shows tinners' streamworkings cutting an intricate maze into the Dartmoor landscape. The pattern of spoil heaps is evidence of the methodical process by which the tinners followed the tin-bearing gravel along the stream beds, throwing up the waste behind them as they progressed. The photo shows the valley of the Ivy Tor Water (Ladybrook) near Belstone.

Below: The view from the Warren House Inn looking towards the distant snowy slopes of Hookney Tor and Grimspound. The deep gullies left by the miners still scar the landscape even though it is more than a century since the miners were here.

Tinners' caches, also known as beehive huts, were used by tinners to store their tools etc. Found across the moor wherever streaming activity took place, they take a great variety of forms and are easily confused with other artefacts, and even natural rock features. Top left: Burnard's c.1890 photograph of a tinner's cache at Deep Swincombe. Top right: Cache at Stonetor Brook. Above: The cache at Downing's House, in the Erme Valley.

A group of children clamber on the edge of the wheel pit in front of the remains of the 36 foot water wheel at Drylake, part of the Henroost mine workings, although fallen into disrepair at the time this photograph was taken c.1910.

Left: Remains of the mine's dressing floor at Hexworthy.

Below: A photograph c.1920 showing the mine workings surrounding the ruined mine building at Hexworthy. The gullies, pits and spoil heaps reveal the extent to which mining ravaged the Dartmoor landscape.

Robert Burnard's annotated Ordnance Survey map of 1886 includes five former mining sites within around one square kilometre, a stark indicator of the density of mining activity across the moor as a whole. The mines marked are: A: Gobbett. B: Hexworthy. C: Dry Lake. D: Hooten Wheals. E: Henroost. Inset: The water wheel at Henroost.

A postcard photograph of Great Rock Mine which stood above the Teign Valley at Hennock. The whole area was rich in minerals with tin, silver, lead-zinc, copper, manganese and barytes being among the ores found here. Great Rock, elsewhere described as Devon's last metal mine, was taken up under that name in 1902, working until its closure in 1969. Ramsley (below) is said to be the last mine in England worked exclusively for copper, was opened as Ramsley Hill Mine in the 1850s and finally abandoned in 1909.

The age of industrial mining largely bypassed Dartmoor and remains of the great mine engine houses and their chimney stacks, so familiar in the Cornish landscape, are few and far between on the moor. Many that were built are long demolished, their beam engines sold to other mines, or scrapped. Clockwise from top left: A solitary stack remains at Ramsley Mine; Druid copper mine already a ruin in 1913; Wheal Betsy Mine, now a scheduled monument; Silverbrook lead-zinc mine, Ilsington.

We imagine early mining was exclusively a male occupation but in the Second World War the women of the villages close to Hemerdon Bal tungsten mine took over work formerly done by men. These photos are of women from nearby Sparkwell who worked shifts at the mine during the war years when tungsten was vital to the war effort.

Below: Two women workers at Great Rock Mine, Hennock in 1945. They stand in the mill where the ore was crushed and passed through tubs and sluices to remove the waste rock.

Discovered in 1867 both tin and tungsten were mined at Hemerdon Bal, also known as Drakelands Mine. Tungsten was essential for the armaments industry and in the making of armour plate and the mine came into its own in the last years of the First World war, producing 16 000 tons of ore.

Having closed between the wars, the mine was reopened in 1943 only to close again at the end of the Second World War. The photograph above was taken towards the end of 1945, the extensive opencast workings just seen upper left and the mill buildings, centre, that were capable of treating 300 tons of ore each day.

As it had always been an open-cast operation there were expensive environmental considerations to be taken into account in reopening the mine, but in 2014 after many years of study, an Australian Company, Wolf Minerals, began operations once again but failed to make it a commercial success and the mine closed in 2018. At the time of writing plans are going ahead to recommence mining at the site.

Shaft headframe and winding engine house at Kelly Mine, Lustleigh. Replicas here are intended to represent what a typical early twentieth century Westcountry small mining installation would look like. The mine is not open to the public except by appointment through the Kelly Mine Preservation Society (www.kellymine.co.uk). Thanks are due to David Allen of the KMPS who compiled the following pages.

NB Former mine sites can offer danger to the walker and care should be taken near former shafts and gullies. Many sites are on private land and are not open to public access without permission.

KELLY MINE, LUSTLEIGH
Recovery and Restoration of a Dartmoor Mine

Although not a tin mine, Kelly mine demands space in this book for it is the only site on the moor that remains to provide a graphic illustration of how metal mining was carried out during the latter years of the industrial mining period. The mineral worked is micaceous haematite, a form of iron. The earliest reference to Kelly Mine is in 1797 when the processed ore was used as a 'pounce mixture' used for drying ink. Although not generally suited for iron making recent finds at the site suggests that some early, possibly very early, iron smelting also took place. The first 'official' mining dates from 1877 by which time micaceous haematite was used in the manufacture of corrosion-resistant paint, the aptly named 'battleship grey'.

The ore processing essentially involved the separation of the valuable material from the waste by washing. Larger fragments being broken initially by hammers and subsequently by mechanical crushing in stamps. The mine has always been water powered. The present mine layout dates back to just after the First World War when the processing mill was enlarged and modernised. The original waterwheel driving the stamps was replaced by a water turbine which as well as driving the crushing machinery powered a winch for haulage on the tramway incline and a compressor for powering rock drills underground.

Although the mine closed in 1951 much of the equipment and mining apparatus remains, thanks in large part to the Kelly Mine Preservation Society who, since 1985, have been restoring the mine site. The site very much retains the atmosphere of what it was like for the men who worked here and is a tangible part of Dartmoor's mining heritage, celebrating all those miners who went before.

A mine tram stands inside the entrance to Bottom Adit during an Open Day demonstration.

Above: The mine tramway: The right hand line goes to the shaft; the centre line descends the incline to Bottom Adit and the left hand line runs onto a waste dump.

The Kelly mine trams provided when the mine was modernized are of unusual design with the body mounted on a pedestal and turntable so that it can rotate through 360 degrees and be tipped in any direction.

Above: A replica sheet metal body with original ironwork and with the turntable mounted on an original steel chassis.

Right: A mainly original timber body, possibly replacing a metal one, with the turntable mechanism mounted on a wooden chassis.

After breaking larger fragments with hammers the ore was processed in the washing strips where the micaceous haematite was separated from the waste and carried through a sieve to settling tanks as a slurry, larger fragments caught by the sieve were sent to the stamps for crushing and further washing.

The outside of the processing mill which contains the water powered machinery. The re-instated waterwheel is just seen alongside the building, top right. The pale grey building, top left, is the 'miners dry' or mess hut where a change of clothes was kept by a stove.

Inside the processing mill: Four heads of Californian stamps on the left; a set of Miniature Cornish stamps to the right with drive wheel from the waterwheel coming in through the wall. The water turbine is below the pulley wheel above the steps in the centre.

The upper floor in the processing mill with an early Ingersoll compressor on the left and a winch for hauling trams on the incline bottom right. These, plus the Californian stamps are driven by belting and line shafting, powered by the water turbine, but replaced by a Blackstone oil engine when the water supply is poor in the summer months.

The 'new' waterwheel re-instated in the original wheelpit alongside the processing mill. The outer rims of the wheel, the shrouds, are from an original wheel purchased by the Society. The central hub and the timber frame on which it is mounted, the axle, the spokes or arms and the buckets are all new components fabricated for the project. The wheel now powers the replica Cornish stamps. The original wheel would have powered Cornish stamps, replaced by the Californian set when the mill was modernized.

The drying shed and associated waterwheel, photographed at the time the Society took over. The shed roof has completely collapsed, the wheel is overgrown and the water supply launder is missing.

The same view after restoration: The drying shed has a completely new roof structure and the original waterwheel has been refurbished complete with a new launder.

The end of the process. A tramway leads from the mill to the drying shed. A tram on the elevated section tips processed ore into the hatch at the top of the drying shed.

Interior of the drying shed. Floor made from iron plate with underfloor heating for drying ore to the right. The drive from the waterwheel on the wall powers a mechanical sieve and elevator which in turn feeds the finished ore into a hopper for filling barrels ready for shipment.

Appendix 1
Jurats Sworn in at Crockern Tor September 1494

CHAGFORD

John Wolcot of Chudlegh
John Brabon
Thomas Staplehyll
Wyllyam Ryse
John Wyddon
Robart Foxforde
Robart Wanell
Wyllyam Furselande
Robart Windeyate
Rycharde Wratt
John Nucombe. Jun ,
Wyllyam Nose worthey
Thomas Myller
Wyllyam Caselegh
Wyllyam Fursse
Wyllyam Denbolde
Alexander Wekes
Thomas Batyshyll
Thomas Tomlyn
John Aysshe
Rycharde Crote
Wyllyam Mowry
Galfridus Loskey
John Smyth (corser)

ASHBURTON

Rycharde Hamlyn
John Vele
John Bonycombe
John Maddocke
Wyllyam Myller
John Baron
Wyllyam Kyng of Hole

John Eyre
Rychard Langworthy
Thomas Mathue
John Eexte of Br ston
Rychard Foxforde
Rycharde Baker
John Wydecombe
Rychard Harte
Wyllyam Wydecombe
John Clyffe
Wyllyam Edwarde
John Saunder
Thomas Gauerocke
Mychell Sperkewyll
John Baker
Robart Tomlyn
Wyllyam Berde

PLYMPTON

Wyllyam at Hele.
Wyllyam Rede
John Beare
Nycolas Brugge
Robarte Batyn
Nycolas Combe
John Hede
Water Adam
Wyllyam Odymer
John Peake at Hele
Wyllyam Tyllam
Wyllyam Forde
Wyllyam Brusey
John Elberton.
Roger Eggecombe
Wylliam Chreston
Jurdan Brugge

Elias Elforde
Androw Wattis
Robart Hamme
John Scobell
Richard Rose
Richard Pomery
William Wyett

TAVISTOCK

Steven Toker
Richard Langesforde
John Chreston
John Leywod
John Glubbe
John Horewyll.
John Cholwyll
John Gye
John Peke of Way
Thomas Forde
John Draper
Thomas Adam.
William Soped
John Hyllan
Wyllyam Gyll
John Eston
Robert Borne
Robert Heyne
Henry Humfrey
Roger Langesforde
Wyllyam Stephen
John Tanner
Henry Haly
John Harte

Appendix 2
The Ashburton Stannary Coinage Roll of 1303

This Roll is the earliest statistical record of mines in existence. It begins *Aspertosi Cunaqiuni ibidem. die Jous proxima Post Jestum Beata Mana Virginis Anno CRXXIMO.* (Queens Remembrancers Miscellances, Mines Tin Coinage Roll 3 lst Ed. I 508).

The following people are listed: Walter Weallying, Richard de Landscoveford, Sarra wife of Gilbert, Hugh Hathen, Galrfidus Cole, Walter Atte Combe, Roger Onelyn, Richard de Middleworth, John Blythebroke, John Hervy, Stephen Wymound, William de Scherewill, Hugh de Corudon, Michael Cole, John Attatorre, Galfridus Mogge, Stephen Mugge.

The following additional names of tinners who had coined at other coinages this year are listed as follows: Bartholemew Attarmede, William Attajeune, John Benet, John Bende, Stephen Cole, Walter de Coomb, Richard Cole, Jude Chileford, Hugh de Fenton, John Laber de Blakedon, Richard Gwynne, John de Harpour, Thomas de Lysington, Richard de Lenstor, Robert le Mythour, Robert Pole, Bart de Pratto, Richard Stenylake, Robert Schire, Walter Smalcomb, Walter Syward, Robert Uppahulle, Walter Withecombe.

Richard the Clerk is mentioned in both lists, and by the next coinage 'Sarra' has become 'the widow of Gilbert'. Later still she is listed as 'Sarra de Holne' (evidently she owned land or rights at Holne).

Title page of the so-called 'Tinners' Charter' printed at Tavistock Abbey in 1533 and containing the various statutes regulating the tin industry.

It begins: 'Here followeth the confirmation of the Charter pertaining to all the tinners within the County of Devonshire, with their statutes also made at Crockern Tor by the whole assent and consent of the said tinners in the year of the reign of our Sovereign Lord King Henry VIII.'

Bibliography

Atkinson, M. Burt, R. White, P. *Dartmoor Mines*, Exeter, 1978.
Baring Gould, Rev Sabine. *A Book of Dartmoor,* 1928 Methuen, 1928.
  Guavas the Tinner, Praxis Books, 2000.
  Songs of the Westcountry, David & Charles, 1974.
Barlow, Prof Frank (Ed.) *Exeter and its Regions*, University Exeter, 1969.
Bauer, Georg. *De re metallica*, London, 1912.
Bellamy, R. *The Book of Postbridge*, Haslgrove, 1999.
Bray, Mrs Anna Eliza. *Descriptions of Parts of Devon bordering Tamar and Tavy, etc.* John Murray, 1836.
  Traditions, Legends, etc. Bohn 1884.
  Borders of Tamar and Tavy, Kent, nd.
  A Peep at the Pixies, Legends of the West, Grant & Griffiths, 1854.
Breton, Rev M. Hugh. *The Forest of Dartmoor, etc.* Hoyten & Cole, 1931.
Brewer, Dave. *Dartmoor Boundary Markers*, Halsgrove, 2002.
Brooks, Tony, *Great Rock, Devon's Last Metal Mine*, Cornish Hillside, 2004.
Brooks, Tony, *Kelly Mine and the Shiny Ore Mines of the Wray Valley*, Exeter, 2016.
Burnard, R. & Prowse, Arthur B. *Dartmoor Place Names, etc.*, Plymouth, 1893.
Burnard, R. *Dartmoor Pictorial Records*, Devon Books, 1986
Burt, Roger. *Devon and Somerset Mines*, Exeter University Press, 1984.
Butler, J. *Dartmoor Atlas of Antiquities, Vols 1-5*, Devon Books, 1991-1996.
Butler, S. *Dartmoor Century I*, Halsgrove, 2000.
Butler, S. *Dartmoor Century II*, Halsgrove, 2001.
Chope, R. Pearse. *Early Tours in Devon & Cornwall*, Exeter, 1918.
Collins, J .H. *Handbook to Mineralogy of Cornwall and Devon*, London, 1871.
Coxhead, J.R.W. *Legends of Devon*, Westward Press, 1954.
Crossing, William. *Crossing's Dartmoor Worker,* David & Charles, 1966.
  Gems in a Granite Setting, 1902, reprinted Devon Books, 1986.
  Guide to Dartmoor, David & Charles, 1965.
  One Hundred Years on Dartmoor, 1902, reprinted Devon Books, 1987.
  The Western Gate of Dartmoor, Homeland Handbooks No. 31.
Dewey, Henry. *British Regional Geology, South West England* HMSO, 1935.
Dines, M.G. *The Metalliferous Mining Regions of S.W. England*, HMSO, 1930.
Edmonds, E.A. et al. *British Regional Geology, S.W. England.* HMSO, 1969.
Evans, Rachel. *Home Scenes of Tavistock and its Vicinity*, London, 1846.
Finberg, H.P.R. *The Stannary of Tavistock*, Trans. Dev. Ass. 81 pp 155-84, 1950.
Finberg, H.P.R. *Tavistock Abbey, etc.*, Cambridge Univ. Press, 1954.
Fox, Aileen. *S.W. England*, Thames & Hudson, 1964.
Francis, E. & Thomas, B. *Yelverton & Surroundings*, Homeland Assn., 1922.
Gerard, Sandy. *Dartmoor*, English Heritage1997.
Gerard, Sandy. *The Early British Tin Industry*, Tempus, 2000.

Gill, Crispin *Dartmoor: A New Study*. David & Charles, 1970.
Gordon, Douglas St Leger. *Devonshire*, Robert Hale, 1950.
   Under Dartmoor Hills, Robert Hale, 1954.
Gordon, Ruth St Leger. *The Witchery and Folklore of Dartmoor*, Robert Hale, 1956.
Gray, Todd et al. *Tudor and Stuart Devon*, Exeter University Press, 1992.
Greeves, T. *Tin MInes and Miners of Dartmoor*, Halsgrove, 2001.
Greeves, T. Newman, P. *The Great Courts of the Devon Tinners*, Dartmoor Tinworking Research Group, 2011.
Hamilton Jenkin, A.K. *Mines of Devon Vol. 1*, David & Charles, 1974.
   Mines of Devon, North and East of Dartmoor, Devon Library Services, 1981.
Hanham, A. (edit) *Churchwardens Accounts Ashburton 1479–1580*, D & C Record Soc. Exeter, 1970.
Harris, Helen *Industrial Archaelogy of Dartmoor*, David & Charles, 1968.
Harvey, A. & Gordon, D. St Leger. *Dartmoor*, Collins, 1962.
Hayter-Hames, Jane. *A History of Chagford,* Phillimore, 1981.
Hitchens, F. and Drew, S. *The History of Cornwall*, Helston, 1824.
Hemery, Eric. *High Dartmoor*, Robert Hale, 1983.
Hoskins, W.G. *Devon*, Phillimore, 2003.
   Old Devon, David & Charles, 1966.
Hoskins, W.G. & Finberg, H.P.R. *Devonshire Studies*, Jonathan Cape, 1952.
Hughes, Lt.-Col. G.W.G. *Moretonhampstead*, Devon Assn, 1954.
James, Miss D. *Belstone, Parish past and present.*, Winchester 1911.
Kelly Mine Preservation Society. *Kelly Mine*, 2014.
Le Messurier, B.. *The Phillpotts Peat Passes of N. Dartmoor*, Trans. Dev. Ass., 1965.
Lewis, G.R. *The Stannaries*, Oxford University Press,1908.
Minchinton, Walter. *Devon at Work*, David & Charles, 1974.
Page, J.L.W. *An Exploration of Dartmoor and its Antiquities*, London, 1889.
Pennington, Robert. *Stannary Law*, David & Charles, 1973.
Perkins, J. W. *Geology of Dartmoor & the Tamar Valley*, David & Charles,1984.
Pike, Revd John. *Observations on the Scenery and Antiquities of the Neighbourhood of Moreton Hampstead and on the Forest of Dartmoor*, Exeter, 1823.
Pryce, William, *Mineralogia Cornubiensis,* Simpkin Marshall, 1893.
King, Richard John. *The Forest of Dartmoor & its Borders*, London. 1856.
Lewis, George Randall. *The Stannaries: A Study of the English Tin Miner*, Harvard Univ. Press. Camb. Mass. U.S.A.
Martin, E.W. *The Shearers and the Shorn*, Routledge & Kegan Paul,1965.
Omerod, G. W. *Archaeological Memoirs Relating of East of Dartmoor,* Exeter, 1876.
   Notes on Rude Stone Remains Situate on the Easterly Side of Dartmoor, Exeter, 1876.
Page, Hugh E. *Rambles in South Devon*, Great Western Railway, London, 1932.
Page, J.H. Warden. *An Exploration of Dartmoor & its Antiquities with some Account of its Borders*, Seeley & Co. London, 1889.
Pearce, Thomas. *The Laws & Customs of the Stannaries in the Counties of Cornwall & Devon, Part II Devon,* London, 1725.
Pilkington, Francis. *Ashburton: The Dartmoor Town,* Devon Books, 1978.
Radford, C.A. *Lydford Castle Devon*, H.M. Offices of Works London, 1936.

Richardson, P.H.G. *Mines of Dartmoor & the Tamar Valley*, Devon Books, 1995.
Rowe Revd Samuel. *A Perambulation. of the Ancient & Royal Forestry of Dartmoor*, Plymouth, 1848.
Royse, Rev W.H. Harvey *Holne: Dartmoor*, London, 1920.
Stanier, Peter. *Mines of Cornwall and Devon*, Twelveheads Press, 1998.
Stephan, Dom John *Ashburton in Catholic Days*, privately printed Buckfast, nd.
 A History of Buckfast Abbey, Burleigh Press Bristol, nd.
Torr, Cecil. *Small Talk at Wreyland*, Cambridge University Press, 1918.
Warne, A. *Church & Society in Eighteenth Century Devon*, David & Charles, 1969.
Woods, Stephen. *Dartmoor Stone*, Devon Books,1998.
Woods, Stephen. *Dartmoor Farm*, Halsgrove, 2003.
Worth, R. Hansford. *Worth's Dartmoor*, David & Charles, 1967.
Worthy, Charles. *Ashburton & its Neighbourhood*, Ashburton, 1875.

TAILPIECE

Kelly miners in front of the mill and flat rod pumping machinery in 1907. The photograph has caused some controversy as to its exact location and is included here as it highlights one of the problems associated with digitising old photographs, particularly from original negatives, as many of the Dartmoor Trust Archive photographs are. In this case the photograph above has been reproduced in complete horizontal reversal from its formerly accepted view. While some are adamant that this is incorrect, others argued that the 'reversed' view above makes more sense of the mine site from the evidence available today.